A PLEASANT CONCEITED
HISTORIE, CALLED

The Taming of a Shrew

SHAKESPEAREAN ORIGINALS:
FIRST EDITIONS

A PLEASANT CONCEITED
HISTORIE, CALLED
The Taming of a Shrew

EDITED AND INTRODUCED BY
GRAHAM HOLDERNESS AND BRYAN LOUGHREY

First published 1992 by
Harvester Wheatsheaf,
Campus 400, Maylands Avenue
Hemel Hempstead
Hertfordshire HP2 7EZ
A division of
Simon & Schuster International Group

Designed by Geoff Green

Typeset in 11pt Bembo
by Photoprint, Torquay, Devon

Printed & bound by Antony Rowe Ltd, Eastbourne

Transferred to digital print on demand, 2003

British Library Cataloguing in Publication Data

A catalogue record for this book
is available from the British Library.

ISBN   0-7450-1103-9 (hbk)
ISBN   0-7450-1104-7 (pbk)

Contents

General Introduction

T H I S series puts into circulation single annotated editions of early modern play-texts whose literary and theatrical histories have been overshadowed by editorial practices dominant since the eighteenth century.

The vast majority of Shakespeare's modern readership encounters his works initially through the standard modernised editions of the major publishing houses, whose texts form the basis of innumerable playhouse productions and classroom discussions. While these textualisations vary considerably in terms of approach and detail, the overwhelming impression they foster is not of diversity but uniformity: the same plays are reprinted in virtually identical words, within a ubiquitous, standardised format. Cumulatively, such texts serve to constitute and define a particular model of Shakespeare's work, conjuring up a body of writing which is given and stable, handed down by the author like holy writ. But the canonical status of these received texts is ultimately dependent not upon a divine creator, but upon those editorial mediations (rendered opaque by the discursive authority of the very texts they ostensibly serve) that shape the manner in which Shakespeare's works are produced and reproduced within contemporary culture.

Many modern readers of Shakespeare, lulled by long-established editorial traditions into an implicit confidence in the object of their attention, probably have little idea of what a sixteenth-century printed play-text actually looked like. Confronted with an example, she or he could be forgiven for recoiling before the intimidating display of linguistic and visual strangeness – antique type, non-standardised spelling, archaic orthographic conventions, unfamiliar and irregular speech prefixes, oddly placed stage directions, and

[1]

possibly an absence of Act and scene divisions. 'It looks more like Chaucer than Shakespeare,' observed one student presented with a facsimile of an Elizabethan text, neatly calling attention to the peculiar elisions through which Shakespeare is accepted as modern, while Chaucer is categorised as ancient. A student reading Chaucer in a modern translation knows that the text is a contemporary version, not a historical document. But the modern translations of Shakespeare which almost universally pass as accurate and authentic representations of an original – the standard editions – offer themselves as simultaneously historical document and accessible modern version – like a tidily restored ancient building.

The earliest versions of Shakespeare's works existed in plural and contested forms. Some nineteen of those plays modern scholars now attribute to Shakespeare (together with the non-dramatic verse) appeared in cheap quarto format during his life, their theatrical provenance clearly marked by an emphasis upon the companies who owned and produced the plays rather than the author.[1] Where rival quartos of a play were printed, these could contrast starkly: the second quarto of *Hamlet* (1604), for example, is almost double the length of its first quarto (1603) predecessor and renames many of the leading characters. In 1623, Shakespeare's colleagues Heminges and Condell brought out posthumously the prestigious and expensive First Folio, the earliest collected edition of his dramatic works. This included major works, such as *Macbeth*, *Antony and Cleopatra*, and *The Tempest* which had never before been published. It also contained versions of those plays, with the exception of *Pericles*, which had earlier appeared in quarto, versions which in some cases differ so markedly from their notional predecessors for them to be regarded not simply as variants of a single work, but as discrete textualisations independently framed within a complex and diversified project of cultural production; perhaps, even, in some senses, as separate plays. In the case of *Hamlet*, for example, the Folio includes some eighty lines which are not to be found in the second quarto, yet omits a fragment of around 230 lines which includes Hamlet's final soliloquy,[2] and far greater differences exist between certain other pairings.

This relatively fluid textual situation continued throughout the seventeenth century. Quartos of individual plays continued to appear sporadically, usually amended reprints of earlier editions, but occasionally introducing new works, such as the first publication of Shakespeare and Fletcher's *The Two Noble Kinsmen* (1634), a play which was perhaps excluded from the Folio on the basis of its collaborative status.[3] The title of another work written in collaboration with Fletcher, *Cardenio*, was entered on the Stationer's Register of 1653, but it appears not to have been published and the play is now lost. The First Folio proved a commercial success and was reprinted in 1632, although again amended in detail. In 1663, a third edition appeared which assigned to Shakespeare *Pericles* and six other plays which are now generally regarded as apocryphal: *The London Prodigall, Locrine, The Yorkshire Tragedy, Sir John Oldcastle, The Puritan,* and *Thomas Lord Cromwell.* These attributions, moreover, were accepted uncritically by the 1685 Fourth Folio.

The assumptions underlying seventeenth-century editorial practice, particularly the emphasis that the latest edition corrects and subsumes all earlier editions, is rarely explicitly stated, but is graphically illustrated by the Bodleian Library's decision to sell off as surplus to requirements the copy of the First Folio it had acquired in 1623 as soon as the enlarged 1663 edition came into its possession.[4] Eighteenth-century editors continued to work within this tradition. Rowe set his illustrated critical edition from the 1685 Fourth Folio, introducing further emendations and modernisations. Alexander Pope used Rowe as the basis of his own text, but he 'corrected' this liberally, partly on the basis of variants contained within the twenty-eight quartos he catalogued but more often relying on his own intuitive judgement, maintaining that he was merely 'restoring' Shakespeare to an original purity which had been lost through 'arbitrary Additions, Expunctions, Transpositions of scenes and lines, Confusions of Characters and Persons, wrong application of Speeches, corruptions of innumerable passages'[5] introduced by actors. Although eighteenth-century editors disagreed fiercely over the principles of their task, all of them concurred in finding corruption at every point of textual transmission (and in Capell's case, composition), and sought the restoration of a perceived poetic genius: for Theobald, Warburton, Johnson and Steevens, 'The multiple sources of corruption justified editorial intervention; in principle at least, the edition that had received the most editorial

[3]

attention, the most recent edition, was the purest because the most purified.'⁶

The conception of the editorial function was decisively challenged in theory and practice by Edmund Malone, who substituted the principles of archaeology for those of evolution. For Malone, there could be only one role for an editor: to determine what Shakespeare himself had written. Those texts which were closest to Shakespeare in time were therefore the only true authority; the accretions from editorial interference in the years which followed the publication of the First Folio and early quartos had to be stripped away to recover the original. Authenticity, that is, was to be based on restoration understood not as improvement but as rediscovery. The methodology thus offered the possibility that the canon of Shakespeare's works could be established decisively, fixed for all time, by reference to objective, historical criteria. Henceforth, the text of Shakespeare was to be regarded, potentially, as monogenous, derived from a single source, rather than polygenous.

Malone's influence has proved decisive to the history of nineteenth- and twentieth-century bibliographic studies. Despite, however, the enormous growth in knowledge concerning the material processes of Elizabethan and Jacobean book production, the pursuit of Shakespeare's original words sanctioned a paradoxical distrust of precisely those early texts which Malone regarded as the touchstone of authenticity. Many assumed that these texts must themselves have been derived from some kind of authorial manuscript, and the possibility that Shakespeare's papers lay hidden somewhere exercised an insidious fascination upon the antiquarian imagination. Libraries were combed, lofts ransacked, and graves plundered, but the manuscripts have proved obstinately elusive, mute testimony to the low estimate an earlier culture had placed upon them once performance and publication had exhausted their commercial value.

Undeterred, scholars attempted to infer from the evidence of the early printed texts the nature of the manuscript which lay behind them. The fact that the various extant versions differed so consider- ably from each other posed a problem which could only be partially resolved by the designation of some as 'Bad Quartos', and therefore non-Shakespearean; for even the remaining 'authorised' texts varied between themselves enormously, invariably in terms of detail and often in terms of substance. Recourse to the concept of manuscript authenticity could not resolve the difficulty, for such a manuscript simply does not exist.[7] Faced with apparent textual anarchy, editors sought solace in Platonic idealism: each variant was deemed an imperfect copy of a perfect (if unobtainable) paradigm. Once again, the editor's task was to restore a lost original purity, employing compositor study, collation, conflation and emendation.[8]

Compositor study attempts to identify the working practices of the individuals who set the early quartos and the Folio, and thus differentiate the non-Shakespearean interference, stripping the 'veil of print from a text' and thus attempting 'to recover a number of precise details of the underlying manuscript'.[9] Collation, the critical comparison of different states of a text with a view to establishing the perfect condition of a particular copy, provided systematic classification of textual variations which could be regarded as putative corruptions. Emendation allows the editor to select one of the variations thrown up by collation and impose it upon the reading of the selected control text, or where no previous reading appeared satisfactory, to introduce a correction based upon editorial judgement. Conflation is employed to resolve the larger scale divergences between texts, so that, for example, the Folio *Hamlet* is often employed as the control text for modern editions of the play, but since it 'lacks' entire passages found only in the second quarto, these are often grafted on to the former to create the fullest 'authoritative' text.

The cuts to the Folio *Hamlet* may reflect, however, not a corruption introduced in the process of transmission, but a deliberate alteration to the text authorised by the dramatist himself. In recent years, the proposition that Shakespeare revised his work and that texts might therefore exist in a variety of forms has attracted considerable support. The most publicised debate has centred on the relationship of the quarto *History of King Lear* and the Folio *Tragedy of King Lear*.[10] The editors of the recent Oxford Shakespeare have broken new ground by including both texts in their one-volume edition on the grounds that the *Tragedy* represents an authorial revision of the earlier *History*, which is sufficiently radical to justify classifying it as a separate play. Wells and Taylor founded their revisionist position upon a recognition of the fact that

Shakespeare was primarily a working *dramatist* rather than literary author and that he addressed his play-texts towards a particular audience of theatrical professionals who were expected to flesh out the bare skeleton of the performance script: 'The written text of any such manuscript thus depended upon an unwritten para-text which always accompanied it: an invisible life-support system of stage directions, which Shakespeare could expect his first audience to supply, or which those first readers would expect Shakespeare himself to supply orally.'[11] They are thus more open than many of their predecessors to the possibility that texts reflect their theatrical provenance and therefore that a plurality of authorised texts may exist, at least for certain of the plays.[12] They remain, however, firmly author centred – the invisible life-support system can ultimately always be traced back to the dramatist himself and the plays remain under his parental authority.[13]

What, however, if it were not Shakespeare but the actor Burbage who suggested, or perhaps insisted on, the cuts to *Hamlet*? Would the Folio version of the play become unShakespearean? How would we react if we *knew* that the Clown spoke 'More than is set down' and that his ad libs were recorded? Or that the King's Men sanctioned additions by another dramatist for a Court performance? Or that a particular text recorded not the literary script of a play but its performance script? Of course, in one sense we cannot know these things. But drama, by its very nature, is overdetermined, the product of multiple influences simultaneously operating across a single site of cultural production. Eyewitness accounts of performances of the period suggest something of the provisionality of the scripts Shakespeare provided to his theatrical colleagues:

> After dinner on the 21st of september, at about two o'clock, I went with my companions over the water, and in the strewn roof-house saw the tragedy of the first Emperor Julius with at least fifteen characters very well acted. At the end of the comedy they danced according to their custom with extreme elegance. Two in men's clothes and two in women's gave this performance, in wonderful combination with each other.[14]

This passage offers what can seem a bizarre range of codes; the strewn roof-house, well-acted tragedy, comic aftermath and elegant transvestite dance, hardly correspond to the typology of Shakespearean drama our own culture has appropriated. The Swiss tourist Thomas Platter was in fact fortunate to catch the curious custom of the jig between Caesar and the boy dressed as Caesar's wife, for by 1612 'all Jigs, Rhymes and Dances' after plays had been 'utterly abolished' to prevent 'tumults and outrages whereby His Majesty's Peace is often broke'.[15] Shakespeare, however, is the 'author' of the spectacle Platter witnessed only in an extremely limited sense; in this context the dramatist's surname functions not simply to authenticate a literary masterpiece, but serves as a convenient if misleading shorthand term alluding to the complex material practices of the Elizabethan and Jacobean theatre industry.[16] It is in the latter sense that the term is used in this series.

Modern theoretical perspectives have destabilised the notion of the author as transcendent subject operating outside history and culture. This concept is in any event peculiarly inappropriate when applied to popular drama of the period. It is quite possible that, as Terence Hawkes argues, 'The notion of a single "authoritative" text, immediately expressive of the plenitude of its author's mind and meaning, would have been unfamiliar to Shakespeare, involved as he was in the collaborative enterprise of dramatic production and notoriously unconcerned to preserve in stable form the texts of most of his plays.'[17] The script is, of course, an integral element of drama, but it is by no means the only one. This is obvious in forms of representation, such as film, dependent on technologies which emphasise the role of the *auteur* at the expense of that of the writer. But even in the early modern theatre, dramatic realisation depended not just upon the scriptwriter,[18] but upon actors, entrepreneurs, promptbook keepers, audiences, patrons, etc. in fact, the entire wide range of professional and institutional interests constituting the theatre industry of the period.

Just as the scriptwriter cannot be privileged over all other influences, nor can any single script. It is becoming clear that within Elizabethan and Jacobean culture, around each 'Shakespeare' play there circulated a wide variety of texts, performing different theatrical functions and adopting different shapes in different contexts of production. Any of these contexts may be of interest to the modern reader. The so-called Bad Quartos, for example, are generally marginalised as piratically published versions based upon

[7]

the memorial reconstructions of the plays by bit-part actors. But even if the theory of memorial reconstruction is correct (and it is considerably more controversial than is generally recognised[19]), these quarto texts would provide a unique window on to the plays as they were originally performed and open up exciting opportunities for contemporary performance.[20] They form part, that is, of a rich diversity of textual variation which is shrouded by those traditional editorial practices which have sought to impose a single, 'ideal' paradigm.

In this series we have sought to build upon the pioneering work of Wells and Taylor, albeit along quite different lines. They argue, for example, that

> The lost manuscripts of Shakespeare's work are not the fiction of an idealist critic, but particular material objects which happen at a particular time to have existed, and at another particular time to have been lost, or to have ceased to exist. Emendation does not seek to construct an ideal text, but rather to restore certain features of a lost material object (that manuscript) by correcting certain apparent deficiencies in a second material object (this printed text) which purports to be a copy of the first. Most readers will find this procedure reasonable enough.[21]

The important emphasis here is on the relative status of the two forms, manuscript and printed text: the object of which we can have direct knowledge, the printed text, is judged to be corrupt by conjectural reference to the object of which we can by definition have no direct knowledge, the uncorrupted (but non-existent) manuscript. This corresponds to no philosophical materialism we have encountered. The editors of *Shakespearean Originals* reject the claim that it is possible to construct a rehabilitated text reflecting a form approximating Shakespeare's artistic vision.[22] Instead we prefer to embrace the early printed texts as authentic material objects, the concrete forms from which all subsequent editions ultimately derive.

We therefore present within this series particular textualisations of plays which are not necessarily canonical or indeed even written by *William Shakespeare, Gent*, in the traditional sense; but which nevertheless represent important facets of Shakespearean drama. In the same way that we have rejected the underlying principles of

[8]

traditional editorial practice, we have also approached traditional editorial procedures with extreme caution, preferring to let the texts speak for themselves with a minimum of editorial mediation. We refuse to allow speculative judgements concerning the exact contribution of the various individuals involved in the production of a given text the authority to license alterations to that text, and as a result relegate compositor study and collation[23] to the textual apparatus rather than attempt to incorporate them into the text itself through emendation.

It seems to us that there is in fact no philosophical justification for emendation, which foregrounds the editor at the expense of the text. The distortions introduced by this process are all too readily incorporated into the text as holy writ. Macbeth's famous lines, for example, 'I dare do all that may become a man / Who dares do more is none,' on closer inspection turn out to be Rowe's. The Folio reads, 'I dare do all that may become a man / Who dares no more is none.' There seems to us no pressing reason whatsoever to alter these lines,[24] and we prefer to confine all such editorial speculation to the critical apparatus. The worst form of emendation is conflation. It is now widely recognised that the texts of the *The Historie of King Lear* (1608) and *The Tragedie of King Lear* (1623) differ so markedly that they must be considered as two distinct plays and that the composite *King Lear* which is reproduced in every twentieth-century popular edition of the play is a hybrid which grossly distorts both the originals from which it is derived. We believe that the case of *Lear* is a particularly clear example of a general proposition: that *whenever* distinct textualisations are conflated, the result is a hybrid without independent value. It should therefore go without saying that all the texts in this series are based upon single sources.

The most difficult editorial decisions we have had to face concern the modernisation of these texts. In some senses we have embarked upon a project of textual archaeology and the logic of our position points towards facsimile editions. These, however, are already available in specialist libraries, but they are there marginalised by those processes of cultural change which have rendered them alien and forbidding. Since we wish to challenge the hegemony of standard editions by circulating the texts within this series as

[9]

widely as possible, we have aimed at 'diplomatic' rather than facsimile status and have modernised those orthographic and printing conventions (such as long s, positional variants of u and v, i and j, ligatures and contractions) which are no longer current and likely to confuse. We do so, however, with some misgiving, recognising that as a result certain possibilities open to the Elizabethan reader are thereby foreclosed. On the other hand, we make no attempt to standardise such features as speech prefixes and *dramatis personae*, or impose conventions derived from naturalism, such as scene divisions and locations, upon the essentially fluid and non-naturalistic medium of the Elizabethan theatre. In order that our own editorial practice should be as open as possible we provide as an appendix a sample of the original text in photographic facsimile. The introductory essay attempts to view the play as a work of art in its own right rather than as an analogue to the received text, pointing towards those recent theoretical formulations which have validated its status and where possible to significant theatrical realisations. Annotation is kept deliberately light, but we do try to point out some of the performance possibilities occluded by traditional editorial mediations.

GRAHAM HOLDERNESS AND BRYAN LOUGHREY

NOTES AND REFERENCES

1. The title page of the popular *Titus Andronicus*, for example, merely records that it was 'Plaide by the Right Honourable the Earle of Darbie, Earle of Pembrooke, and Earle of Sussex their Servants', and not until 1598 was Shakespeare's name attached to a printed version of one of his plays, *Love's Labour's Lost*.
2. For a stimulating discussion of the relationship between the three texts of *Hamlet*, see Steven Urkowitz, '"Well-sayd olde Mole". Burying Three *Hamlets* in Modern Editions', in Georgianna Ziegler (ed.), *Shakespeare Study Today* (New York: AMS Press, 1986), pp. 37–70.
3. In the year of Shakespeare's death Ben Jonson staked a far higher claim for the status of the playwright, bringing out the first ever collected edition of English dramatic texts, *The Workes of Beniamin Jonson*, a carefully prepared and expensively produced folio volume. The text of his Roman tragedy *Sejanus*, a play originally written with an unknown collaborator, was carefully revised to preserve the purity of authorial

[10]

input. See Bryan Loughrey and Graham Holderness, 'Shakespearean Features', in Jean Marsden (ed.), *The Appropriation of Shakespeare: Post-Renaissance Reconstructions of the Works and the Myth* (Hemel Hempstead: Harvester Wheatsheaf, 1991), p. 183.

4. F. Madan and G.M.R. Turbutt (eds), *The Original Bodleian Copy of the First Folio of Shakespeare* (Oxford: Oxford University Press, 1905), p. 5.

5. Cited in D. Nicol Smith, *Eighteenth Century Essays* (Oxford: Oxford University Press, 1963), p. 48.

6. Margareta de Grazia, *Shakespeare Verbatim* (Oxford: Oxford University Press, 1991), p. 62. De Grazia provides the fullest and most stimulating account of the important theoretical issues raised by eighteenth-century editorial practice.

7. Unless the Hand D fragment of 'The Booke of Sir Thomas Moore' (British Library Harleian MS 7368) really is that of Shakespeare. See Stanley Wells and Gary Taylor, *William Shakespeare: A Textual Companion* (Oxford: Oxford University Press, 1987), pp. 461–7.

8. See Margareta de Grazia, 'The essential Shakespeare and the material book', *Textual Practice*, vol. 2, no. 1, spring 1988.

9. Fredson Bowers, 'Textual Criticism', in O.J. Campbell and E.G. Quinn (eds), *The Reader's Encyclopedia of Shakespeare* (New York: Methuen, 1966), p. 869.

10. See, for example, Gary Taylor and Michael Warren (eds), *The Division of the Kingdoms* (Oxford: Oxford University Press, 1983).

11. Stanley Wells and Gary Taylor, *William Shakespeare: A Textual Companion* (Oxford, Oxford University Press, 1987), p. 2.

12. See, for example, Stanley Wells, 'Plural Shakespeare', *Critical Survey*, vol. 1, no. 1, spring 1989.

13. See, for example, *Textual Companion*, p. 69.

14. Thomas Platter, a Swiss physician who visited London in 1599 and recorded his playgoing; cited in *The Reader's Encyclopaedia*, p. 634. For a discussion of this passage see Richard Wilson, *Julius Caesar: A Critical Study* (Harmondsworth: Penguin, 1992), chapter 3.

15. E.K. Chambers, *The Elizabethan Stage* (Oxford: Oxford University Press, 1923) pp. 340–1.

16. The texts of the plays sometimes encode the kind of stage business Platter recorded. The epilogue of *2 Henry IV*, for example, is spoken by a dancer who announces that 'My tongue is weary; when my legs are too, I will bid you good night . . .'

17. Terence Hawkes, *That Shakespeherian Rag* (London: Methuen, 1986), p. 75.

18. For a discussion of Shakespeare's texts as dramatic scripts, see Jonathan

Bate, 'Shakespeare's Tragedies as working scripts', *Critical Survey*, vol. 3, no. 2, 1991, pp. 118–27.

19. See, for example, Random Cloud [Randall McCleod], 'The Marriage of Good and Bad Quartos', *Shakespeare Quarterly*, vol. 33, no. 4., pp. 421–30.

20. See, for example, Bryan Loughrey, 'QI in modern performance', in Tom Clayton (ed.), *QI Now* (Minnesota: University of Nebraska Press, 1991) and Nicholas Shrimpton, 'Shakespeare Performances in London and Stratford-Upon-Avon, 1984–5', *Shakespeare Survey 39*, pp. 193–7.

21. *Textual Companion*, p. 60.

22. The concept of authorial intention, which has generated so much debate amongst critics, remains curiously unexamined within the field of textual studies.

23. Charlton Hinman's Norton Facsimile of *The First Folio of Shakespeare* offers a striking illustration of why this should be so. Hinman set out to reproduce the text of the original First Folio, but his collation of the Folger Library's numerous copies demonstrated that 'every copy of the finished book shows a mixture of early and late states of the text that is peculiar to it alone'. He therefore selected from the various editions those pages he believed represented the printer's final intentions and bound these together to produce something which 'has hitherto been only a theoretical entity, an abstraction: *the* First Folio'. Thus the technology which would have allowed him to produce a literal facsimile in fact is deployed to create an ahistorical composite which differs in substance from every single original upon which it is based. See Charlton Hinman, *The First Folio of Shakespeare* (New York: 1968), pp. xiii–xiv.

24. Once the process begins, it becomes impossible to adjudicate between rival conjectural emendations. In this case, for example, Hunter's suggestion that Lady Macbeth should be given the second of these lines seems to us neither more nor less persuasive than Rowe's.

Introduction

THE text contained in this volume is not what we know as
Shakespeare's *The Taming of the Shrew*, modern editions of which
play are all derived from the text printed in the 1623 First Folio
edition of Shakespeare's works. The present text is an edition of
the play published in 1594 under the title *The Taming of a Shrew*,
which has always been denied the authorising signature of 'Shakespeare', and regarded as an earlier version by another dramatist or
as a pirated and corrupt 'memorial reconstruction' of Shakespeare's
The Taming of the Shrew. Yet the version accepted as 'Shakespeare's'
was not published before the First Folio of 1623; contemporary
records hardly seem to distinguish between the two plays; and the
text included in the First Folio was printed by virtue of a copyright
which appears to have related to the earlier published text.

In many ways *A Shrew* is a more interesting text than *The Shrew*
– it contains, for example, a complete theatrical 'framing' device in
the form of the Lord's practical joke on Christopher Slie, where
the 'Shakespearean' text drops Sly and the framing device early in
the play – and from the beginning of this century the 'non-
Shakespearean' text has been used in theatrical practice to complete
the authorised but insufficient 'Shakespearean' play. This new
edition makes *The Taming of a Shrew* available in full, not as a
'source' or 'analogue' or 'memorial reconstruction of a Shakespearean
original', but in its own right as a brilliantly inventive popular
Elizabethan play.

★

Once it became generally accepted by scholars that *The Taming of
a Shrew* should be regarded as a memorial reconstruction of an

[13]

original performance of Shakespeare's *The Taming of the Shrew*, the scholarly obligation became a simple task of invidious comparison, calculated to establish the superiority and originality of the text preserved in the First Folio, and requiring the release of tirades of rhetorical invective against the pirate or pirates responsible for the production of this 'Bad Quarto'.[1]

The Taming of a Shrew is, according to H.J. Oliver, editor of the Oxford Shakespeare edition of *The Taming of the Shrew*,[2] 'clearly inferior' (p. 14), its author 'stupid' (p. 16) and 'inept' (p. 20). Pathetically 'trying to recall phrases he does not even understand' (p. 19), the imbecilic pirate produced a text characterised by 'incompetent versification', 'execrable' blank verse, 'slackness in diction', 'feeble repetition of words', and containing passages 'of no literary merit at all' (p. 20). Brian Morris, editor of the Arden Shakespeare edition of *The Taming of the Shrew*[3] also sees the 1594 text as a reconstruction, 'without adequate recollection' (p. 36) of the original, the blanks of piratical memory padded out with 'limping rhythms' (p. 37) and wretched comic dialogue, 'sorry stuff' (p. 38). Even Ann Thompson, who in the New Cambridge edition of *The Taming of the Shrew*[4] rejects this strategic demonisation of the alternative text, admitting it to be a play 'of considerable interest and merit' (p. 164), seems to endorse the scholarly tradition of comparative evaluation, acknowledging *The Taming of a Shrew* to be 'cruder' than the 'more polished' Shakespearean original, characterised by unnecessarily 'explicit articulation' of plot (p. 166).

In fact many of the detailed comparisons originally offered by scholars like Samuel Hickson, G.I. Duthie and Raymond A. Houk,[5] and subsequently represented for endorsement by editors of the Folio text, will withstand very little serious examination once the Quarto text is addressed as an appropriate object of investigation in its own right. Particular observations alleging inconsistency of dramatic structure, often involving the interpretation of characters' declared intentions, or apparent contradictions in character or audience knowledge of events, can be made against virtually any Elizabethan dramatic text. Such objections depend on anachronistic conceptions of theatrical time and space, and quickly recede in importance when the play is presented (as it is in this edition) without the act and scene divisions subsequently added by editorial interference. Detailed comments made by earlier scholars and regarded as particularly telling by modern editors, often seem merely a matter of wilful misinterpretation. Where Christopher Slie heralds the entrance of Kate, accompanied by Valeria disguised as a music master, with the expostulation 'O brave, heers two fine gentlewomen', scholars have found a clear inconsistency, and postulated incorrectness in the ordering of scenes. But since Christopher Slie misunderstands everything he sees, and since the entire medium of the play is pervaded by conventions of disguise, cross-dressing and gender transformation, the accepted explanation in terms of textual corruption begins to appear wildly improbable.[6]

Stylistic comparisons seem equally unconvincing, their context frequently evincing a remarkable lack of attention to shifts in standards of poetic taste. H.J. Oliver (Oxford Shakespeare *The Taming of the Shrew*), following Samuel Hickson's 1850 essay, questions whether *A Shrew*'s

> As glorious as the morning washt with dew . . .

'could be anything other than a not quite successful attempt to recapture, from *The Shrew*' (p. 15)

> As morning roses newly washt with dew . . .

Most modern readers would surely find in *The Shrew*'s line a trite and conventional conceit, and in the line from *A Shrew* an arresting and vivid metaphorical expression.

To enter into a detailed defence of *The Taming of a Shrew* against this tradition of comparative condemnation cannot, of course, be done without complicity in the established parameters of this bibliographical problematic – piracy, memorial reconstruction, the self-evident inferiority and inauthenticity of a 'stolne, and surreptitious cop[y]'[7]. As Stephen Urkowitz has pointed out, the 'memorial reconstruction' hypothesis itself

> seems to have prevented close examination of the fundamental documents of our literary–dramatic tradition by its practitioners, teachers of literature and performers of plays. Labeling certain texts as 'bad' quartos has removed them from the normal discourse in which such documents would otherwise be included.[8]

Although Urkowitz in this essay leans, like Stanley Wells and Gary Taylor, towards a view of the multiple texts as indications of authorial revision – thus clinging to an umbilical cord firmly attaching the texts to an 'author' – his key emphasis is surely correct: the various surviving printed texts of early modern drama should be accepted as the 'fundamental documents', and should be 'studied for what they are, in and of themselves, rather than solely as pernicious desecrations of Shakespeare's iconic originals' (p. 204).

In fact the scholarly debate around the relationship between *The Taming of the Shrew* and *The Taming of a Shrew* (henceforward *The Shrew* and *A Shrew*) has produced a substantial body of detailed commentary, sufficient to absolve scholars of any allegation that *A Shrew* has not been closely examined. This sustained examination of the Quarto text has, however, caused a noticeable stretching of the normal shape of the Bad Quarto hypothesis, which has to be continually qualified if the evidence of *A Shrew* is to be accommodated. Richard Hosley suggested, in the course of arguing for a Bad Quarto designation for *A Shrew*, that the text would have to be identified as an ' "abnormal" type'[9] of memorial reconstruction. *A Shrew* is so different from *The Shrew* in so many particulars as to raise the possibility that it was not so much badly copied, as not copied at all. Perhaps *The Shrew* was not in fact 'badly' transmitted; and it is certainly not 'bad' in literary and theatrical terms: as Ann Thompson (New Cambridge Shakespeare *The Taming of the Shrew*) affirms, 'The combination of the three plots is a remarkably sophisticated example of dramatic structure for the early 1590s and the detailed execution of parts of the play is also very impressive' (p. 166).

But the most intransigent obstacle confronting the Bad Quarto theory in relation to this text is that it is, in at least one respect, more complete (and therefore more complex and sophisticated) than the Folio text of *The Shrew*. Shakespeare's play in the 'authorised' form of the Folio text contains of Christopher Sly only the two opening scenes know as the 'Induction', and a moment of foregrounding at the end of Act 1, Scene 1: from the second scene of the *Shrew* action, nothing more is seen or heard of the dreaming drunken beggar.[10] In *A Shrew*, by contrast, the Slie-narrative is not

[16]

a prologue but an extended dramatic framework: Slie and his attendants are kept on stage virtually throughout, and are given several further comments on and interventions in the action of the play. This fact alone pushes the Bad Quarto hypothesis into a very tight corner. Either 'Shakespeare's' play in performance had no comprehensive Sly-framework, and the imbecile pirate eked out the gaps in his memory by stumbling accidentally on a brilliant piece of theatrical design: in which case he can hardly any longer be regarded as an imbecile pirate. Or Shakespeare's play did in performance carry a complete Slie-framework: in which case the Bad Quarto is a more accurate record of those performances than the 1623 text, which ought in consistency to be redesignated a 'Bad Folio'.

This edition does not seek to offer a definitive explanation of the provenance of *A Shrew*, or to adjudicate authoritatively on the question of its relationship with Shakespeare's play: but simply to put the play into circulation, for its own sake and in its own right, as an authentic historical document of the Elizabethan theatre, and as a very early instance of the extraordinary theatrical complexity and dramatic multiplicity of the popular Elizabethan drama. It is offered as a 'Shakespearean Original' rather than independently as an anonymous play, since its origins were clearly so closely bound up with those of the Folio play that it can be identified, if not as a work by Shakespeare, certainly as a product of 'Shakespeare' – the shorthand title designating a particular collaborative mechanism of cultural production. This is not to claim that 'Shakespeare wrote *The Taming of A Shrew*' in any of the accepted traditional meanings of that phrase. But we also deny the possibility of any claim that 'Shakespeare wrote' the texts of the Shakespeare canon, if by that assertion is intended a clear, unmediated, direct and controlling relationship between author and text. The basic editorial premise of this edition, as of this series, is that the earliest printed versions, including the 1623 Folio texts (rather than conjecturally reconstructed manuscripts, foul and fair copies, scribal transcripts and prompt-copies) are the authentic historical form in which Shakespearean drama entered modern culture, and should therefore be accepted as the appropriate basis of the modern edition.

★

[17]

Introduction

We have already quoted Ann Thompson's suggestion that the most exciting and innovative feature of *A Shrew*'s dramatic structure is its combination and interrelating of three separate 'plots' or centres of dramatic action. The initial intoxication, expulsion and deception of Christopher Slie provides a context of metadramatic on-stage dramatisation within which the commissioned performance, by strolling players, of 'The Taming of a Shrew' is appropriately established and presented. The inner play itself consists of two interdependent narratives: the courtship, marriage and 'taming' of Kate by Ferando, and the wooing of Kate's two sisters, Emelia and Phylema, by Polidor and his friend Aurelius. Strictly speaking, the entire play could be described as consisting of four separable dimensions, since some of the scenes involving the clowns, Sander and Polidor's Boy, represent a form of inserted comic episode, rather than an organically integrated line of 'subplot' (though the episodes certainly reflect the play's main thematic and theatrical preoccupations).

In general, the four subnarratives are tightly interwoven both by interdependence of dramatic action, consistency of theatrical device and continuity of theme. Since the Christopher Slie action is here a complete, enclosing framework, with the choric observer remaining present throughout, rather than enduring summary banishment after one scene, it provides a continuous, metadramatic perspective on the inner play, illuminating the 'taming' action as a theatrical performance rather than a naturalistically presented social, moral and psychological event. Marginalisation of the Slie-frame – which has often been omitted altogether from productions of the Folio text – converts the play into a naturalistic comedy (with varying degrees of farce) in which issues of marriage and sexual politics are dramatised (with more or less seriousness) by actors presenting themselves as real characters within a convincingly realistic social and domestic setting. Incorporation of the Slie-frame creates an entirely different dramatic medium: for the 'inner play' is designated by that frame as an elaborate hoax – part of a series of tricks calculated to fool a poor man into a temporary illusion of riches and power. The 'Induction' of the Folio text opens up a theatrical perspective in which the action of the play is illuminated, by an invigorated sceptical consciousness, as an enacted artifice: only to

[18]

Introduction

close it again, as the inner play ('Catherine and Petruchio') dominates the stage, and memory of that initial alienation-effect inevitably recedes. The entire Slie-frame by contrast confronts the audience with a continual, *unforgettable* reminder that the actors of the *Shrew* play are a fortuitously gathered bunch of travelling players capriciously engaged to enact a whimsical nobleman's practical joke.

Besides establishing a particularly productive context of sustained alienation-effect, *A Shrew*'s Christopher Slie framework broaches all the central themes and preoccupations of the play: class and class distinction; trickery and deception; illusion and theatrical representation; disguise and transformation.

First, the Lord takes advantage of Slie's intoxication to establish the practical joke by means of which the drunk is apparently transformed, by a switch of clothes and a shift of physical environment, into a Lord. The Lord in turn changes himself into a servant, adopting a disguise calculated to render him indistinguishable from the lower orders:

Now take my cloake, and give me one of yours,
Al fellowes now . . .   (p. 44)

The other servants thus become his 'fellowes' (coperpetrators of the practical joke), but also 'fellowes' in a more levelling sense, as the Lord appears to embrace a kind of class solidarity with his companions of the servile fraternity.

The strolling players, who arrive as fortuitously as their counterparts in *Hamlet* ('The fittest time they could have chosen out', p. 45), are also clearly identified as belonging – unlike the courtly professionals of *Hamlet* – to a servile or even vagabond station: they enter, according to the stage direction, 'with packs at their backs' (p. 45). One of the players is identified, by an initial speech prefix, as 'Sander', the company clown, who will play the part of Ferando's man. The players are incorporated by the Lord into the deception practised on Slie, thus making explicit at the outset the link between farcical trickery and theatrical illusion. Their command performance constitutes an additional level of deception for Slie; but is introduced to the audience, by a piece of crude freemasonry addressed by Sander to the Lord, as an extension of the practical joke, an elaboration of the illusory wish-fulfilment fantasy:

1 *The Taming of the Shrew*, Shakespeare Memorial Theatre, 1960, (*left to right*) Bartholomew, Huntsman, Huntsman, Lord, Huntsman, Sly, Huntsman (photo: Angus McBean).

Marrie my lord tis calde The taming of a shrew:
Tis a good lesson for us my lord, for us that are maried men.

(p. 45)

'That's excellent sure', observes the Lord; but the play seems
appropriate to its context of performance not so much in Hamlet's
sense of an 'excellent play',[11] as in the cruder sense of an excellent
moral lesson in the legitimate rights of men and the necessary
subjugation of women.

At the very outset, then, we find a formal linking of the delusion
practised on Christopher Slie, with the persuasive artifice of the
drama itself. For the audience, this introduces a further dimension
to the theatrical spectacle, consisting in the relationship between
what is happening within the stage action, and the theatrical event
itself; between the play and the play's own self-consciousness. The
Slie-framework enables the audience to acquire a self-conscious,
metadramatic awareness of the illusion being offered by the 'taming'
play. This is nowhere more in evidence than in Slie's interventions.
When Aurelius' father the Duke demands that Valeria and Phylotus
be imprisoned, Slie vehemently protests:

> *Slie.* I say wele have no sending to prison.
> *Lord.* My Lord this is but the play, theyre but in jest. (pp. 80–1)

If what the audience in the theatre sees is also 'but the play', the
actors 'but in jest', then it is possible that the 'taming' story itself
is little more than a comic fantasy. At the end of the play, it is
apparent, however, that Slie has failed to grasp this truth, and has
instead absorbed only the self-contained moral lesson proposed
initially by Sander:

> *Slie.* I know now how to tame a shrew . . .
> . . . Ile to my
> Wife presently and tame her too
> And if she anger me. (p. 89)

Since the play represents Slie's acceptance of the doctrine of male
superiority embodied in the 'taming' plot, an obedient complicity
with that same chauvinist ethic on the part of the audience seems
all the more inconceivable.

The romance plot involving the courtship of Emelia and Phylena
by Polidor and Aurelius, echoes all these continuous themes. The

[21]

father of the three daughters, Alfonso, is a wealthy merchant, not a nobleman. Aurelius, son of the Duke of Cestus, has to disguise himself as a member of the merchant class in order to make a socially acceptable offer of marriage. Aurelius confers on his servant Valeria, again by a change of clothes, his own status as son to the Duke (p. 50). Later Valeria is disguised as a music teacher to occupy Kate while the suitors court their ladies. Aurelius recruits a merchant to pose as his father, again passing off Valeria as the Duke's son, a deception which is subverted by the unexpected appearance of the Duke himself. These external transformations undergone by the male suitors are thrown into relief by the much more substantial transformations of the women, from pliable romantic fiancées, dutifully receiving their suitors' courtly addresses, to forceful and independent wives, who refuse to come at their husband's bidding.

The central 'taming' action involving Kate and Ferando intensifies and complicates all these themes. The transformation of Kate from 'shrew' into dutiful wife is accomplished partly by Ferando's continual mutations from one state or condition to another. The persona of tough, cheerful and determined 'shrew-tamer' is varied by the temporary adoption of a romantic courtliness (p. 62), by the assumption of a 'base' costume (reversing Slie's transformation) in order to subvert the wedding ceremony, concluded by an abrupt and inexplicable departure (pp. 61–2); and by the apparent madness he assumes on the visit to his country house (p. 68). The critical moment of Kate's submission/reconciliation is engineered by the elaborate distortion of time and physical reality (the 'sun and moon' episode, p. 78); and a confirmation of the couple's mutuality demonstrated in the episode where Ferando and Kate both lavish on the bewildered Duke an inappropriate litany of courtly homage to the youth and beauty of a woman (pp. 78–9).

Even in the episodic scenes involving the clowns, the same preoccupations prevail. When Sander is left in charge of affairs by Ferando, he immediately assumes a consciousness of superiority which permits him to condescend to Polidor's servant (p. 55). In a later scene the servants threaten one another in a parody of elevated language and chivalric convention (p. 64). The clown Sander adopts a characteristic strategy of teasing and trickery in relation to the hungry Kate (p. 70), and to the Tailor (p. 74). In his attempt to exercise the servant's prerogative of tricking his master, he is however outwitted by Ferando (p. 68).

The multilayered plurality of *A Shrew*'s theatrical design necessarily involved a dispersal of dramatic space, and a diversity of dramatic styles. The first of these characteristics found its natural home on the unlocalised Elizabethan stage. The 'ale-house side' where Slie is discovered sleeping, the exotic combination of commercial centre and classical utopia making up this play's conception of 'Athens', the bizarre hinterland of Ferando's country house, were all imaginatively constructed and deconstructed on that same bare stage. Since space and time were not represented visually, they remained flexible and relative dimensions of dramatic narrative, which could be realised as objectively present, or estranged into fictional distance, by the verbal and gestic codes of the drama. Just as the Christopher Slie framework introduces into the play a fundamental indeterminacy about the relations of reality and illusion: so the unlocalised theatrical practice of the Elizabethan public stage constructed within the dramatic narrative an indeterminate relationship between present and past, the exotic and the immediate, here and now and there and then.

The coexistence within the drama of sharply divergent linguistic registers has been cited as circumstantial evidence of its 'badness':

> the existence of so many various and strongly distinguished styles in this anonymous text might give rise to suspicion of multiple authorship. And the Bad Quarto theory does not rule out the possibility of collaboration between several people in a memorially reconstructed text.[12]

There is, of course, more than a 'suspicion of multiple authorship' – a practice which scarcely requires such indignant dismissal – about a great deal of early modern drama. And it is precisely the capacity of that drama to embrace and integrate such diversity of experience, ideology, genre, convention and language into a complex, overdetermined unity that renders it so rich and interesting a form of cultural production.

Stylistic diversity is virtually announced at the very beginning of the play as a characteristic of its discursive medium:

[23]

Introduction

> *Tapster.*
> You whoreson droonken slave, you had best be gone
> And empty your droonken panch some where else . . .
>
> *Lord.* Now that the gloomie shaddow of the night,
> Longing to view Orions drisling lookes . . .   (p. 43)

The crude, colloquial language of the Slie-action is brought into
particularly sharp juxtaposition by the device of formal quotation:
the Lord's lines are lifted directly from Marlowe's *Dr Faustus*,[13] a
popular and evidently familiar play which is known to have been
in performance in September 1594. The existence within the text
of *A Shrew* of this and several other quotations from Marlowe's
plays has again been assumed as evidence of 'badness', the piratical
memory being, as well as notoriously unscrupulous, eclectically
undiscriminating. Yet the effect here is surely one of ironic
quotation rather than promiscuous pastiche (compare Sander's
jokes about *Dr Faustus* in performance, p. 46). In *Dr Faustus* this
peroration leads to a diabolical incantation: 'Faustus, begin . . .';
here in *A Shrew* it culminates bathetically in a much more banal
exhortation: 'Here break we off our hunting for tonight . . .'
When the Tapster reappears at the end of the play, he no longer
shares with Slie a crude dialect, having absorbed the Lord's capacity
for lofty Marlovian rhetoric:

> *Tapster.* Now that the darkesome night is overpast,
> And dawning day apeares in cristall sky . . .   (p. 88)

Similarly discordant juxtapositions of language occur in any case
regularly through the text of *A Shrew*:

> *Feran.* This humor must I holde me to a while,
> To bridle and hold backe my headstrong wife,
> With curbes of hunger: ease: and want of sleepe,
> Nor sleepe nor meate shall she injoie to night,
> Ile mew her up as men do mew their hawkes,
> And make her gentlie come unto the lure,
> Were she as stuborne or as full of strength
> As were the *Thracian* horse *Alcides* tamde,
> That King *Egeus* fed with flesh of men,
> Yet would I pull her downe and make her come
> As hungry hawkes do flie unto there lure.   *Exit.*

[24]

Introduction

Enter *Aurelius* and *Valeria*.

Aurel. Valeria attend: I have a lovely love,
As bright as is the heaven cristalline,
As faire as is the milkewhite way of Jove,
As chast as *Phoebe* in her sommer sportes,
As softe and tender as the asure downe,
That circles *Cithereas* silver doves.
Her do I meane to make my lovely bride,
And in her bed to breath the sweete content,
That I thou knowst long time have aimed at. (pp. 68–9)

The full ferocity of Ferando's bizarre 'humour' is thrown into
dislocating contrast with Aurelius' conventional romantic sentiment.
Ferando's imagery of darkness and enclosure matches the starlit
open sky of Aurelius' 'heaven cristalline'; the hungry hawk contrasts
with the 'silver doves'; the cruel images of restraint in 'bridle' and
'curbes' are paralleled by the playful liberty of '*Phoebe* in her
sommer sportes'. Ferando's fantasy of the wedding night as a scene
of torture and deprivation contrast with Aurelius' vision of married
bliss: 'in her bed to breath the sweete content'.

At the same time, the underlying sexual metaphor in Ferando's
speech – that of 'feeding' the woman with the man's flesh –
suggests the presence within this violent conception of marriage of
a strong physical dimension, as if Ferando is proposing to deprive
Kate of sex as well as food, to inculcate in her a hunger for sexual
satisfaction rather than a respect for masculine authority. Aurelius'
speech is a typical example of the sentimental romanticism which
dissolves on contact with reality: the play ends with Ferando and
Kate in evident mutuality ('we will to our beds'), but with the
disillusioned romantic heroes at odds with their recalcitrant wives.

Ferando's important soliloquy has, of course, been singled out
as a clear instance of memorial corruption. The Folio text uses
other terms from falconry, particularly the phrase 'man my haggard',
which is a method of training a falcon to come to the lure by starving
it. The Quarto text talks rather of 'mewing' the bird, which involves
confining it to moult, and has nothing to do with either starving or
training the hawk to the lure. Scholars have suggested confusion
here, arising from the pirate's ignorance of hawking terminology.
In fact the version in *A Shrew* makes perfectly good sense: Ferando

[25]

will confine Katherine ('mew her up') and 'make her come' to the lure, two separate operations. I doubt if any reader not concerned with a comparison between the two texts would experience difficulty here at all.

Editors have also obediently followed G.I. Duthie in claiming that the reference to flesh-eating horses is inapposite. H.J. Oliver (Oxford Shakespeare *The Taming of the Shrew*), for example, says: 'The taming of horses by feeding them is a most curious analogue to the taming of haggards by starving them'.[14] But the continuous focus of all this imagery is on flesh eating as a metaphor for sex: the falconer's lure is in this case precisely 'the flesh of men', the penis by means of which Ferando is determined to subdue his wife, to 'pull her downe and make her come' (p. 68). Later, of course, Ferando tantalises the hungry Kate with 'a peece of meate uppon his daggers point' (p. 70).

It is perhaps also worth pointing out that this text's deployment of an imagery of violent restraint –

> To bridle and hold backe my headstrong wife
> With curbes of hunger . . .   (p. 68)

– is much more precise and specific, with its allusions to the 'bridle' and 'curb' (images drawn from horse-riding, but with an echo of the 'scold's bridle'[15]) than the Folio's 'thus I'll curb her mad and headstrong humour'. In that text the metaphor is buried deeply enough to escape comment from any of the *The Shrew*'s modern editors.

★

Leah Marcus has suggested that one of the reasons for *A Shrew*'s exclusion from the Shakespeare canon is that it 'hedges the play's patriarchal message with numerous qualifiers that do not exist in the Folio'.[16] I have argued the same case: but it should at the same time be emphasised that within that alienating frame *A Shrew* probably offers the 'patriarchal message' in a more crude, brutal and violent form than its Folio counterpart. It is precisely in the extremity of contrast between the sceptical detachment of the play's theatrical design, and the cheerful brutality of its 'taming'

2 *The Taming of the Shrew*, Shakespeare Memorial Theatre, 1960, (*above*) Sly, Bartholomew, (*at window*) Prompter, (*below, left to right*) Lucentio, Bianca, Gremio, Tranio, Grumio, Baptista, Hortensio (Shakespeare Centre Library).

narrative, that *A Shrew* produces in terms of sexual politics a remarkably interesting text.

It seems highly improbable that this blunt assertion of patriarchal power, formally subverted in any case by its qualifying narrative frame, could have successfully imposed an ideological uniformity on the popular audience of the Elizabethan public playhouse – confirming the men in the security of their power, requiring dutiful submission from the women. The very sharpness of its sexual politics would seem to make the play provocative and polemical rather than persuasive: offering different kinds of challenge to both genders in the audience.

The subsequent history of the play's reproduction, both as text and theatre, offers further evidence for this view. The formal instability implicit in both the *Shrew* plays can be traced performatively in twentieth-century stage history, or textually through a long series of free adaptations – John Lacey's 1698 comedy *Sauny the Scot* (which brings together Petruchio from *The Shrew* and Sander from *A Shrew*, combining them with a cast of Restoration characters), James Worsdale's 1735 'ballad farce' *A Cure for a Scold*, Edward Garrick's *Catherine and Petruchio* (1756), the Broadway musical *Kiss Me Kate* – a history which discloses a theatrical narrative in a diverse and continual process of reproduction. Restoration and eighteenth-century adaptations were acutely sensitive to the problematical quality of the Shrew-narrative's sexual politics, and modified the text accordingly: either, for example, by omitting the whole of the wife's final speech, or by giving the husband formal expressions of mutual love and reciprocal obligation. James Worsdale's *A Cure for a Scold* has an epilogue in which the actress gratefully drops and distances herself firmly from her role as a wife:

> Well, I must own, it wounds me to the heart
> To act, unwomanly – so mean a part.[17]

There is no comparable internal distantiation of actor from role in the Folio *Shrew*; but there is a parallel detachment of subject from role in the Quarto:

> *Kate.* Why father, what do you meane to do with me,
> To give me thus unto this brainsick man,
> That in his mood cares not to murder me?

> She turnes aside and speakes.
> But yet I will content and marry him,
> For I methinkes have livde too long a maid,
> And match him to, or else his manhoods good.   (p. 53)

Ann Thompson finds the aside 'clumsy' (p. 165); yet it surely indicates that what was formally decoded in *A Cure for a Scold* was already encoded in the Quarto text.

The most conclusive illustration of this argument is to be found in the completeness of the Christopher Slie framework in *A Shrew*. If Slie was to be retained on stage throughout, the dramatic structure constituted by this provision of an on-stage audience alters the nature of the theatrical event. If the play is in one sense a delusion practised on Christopher Slie, then it may be recognised as a delusion practised on the audience as well. When Slie at the end of *A Shrew* proposes to go off and tame his wife, the crudity of the taming plot is clearly acknowledged and exposed to the knowledge of the audience. In 1594 the play might well have been performed in the self-reflexive, metadramatic and alienatory manner of Brecht's epic theatre, delivering its patriarchal message with appropriate detachment, distancing and irony to an audience highly sceptical of such propagandist rhetoric. The play might well have been offered as a challenge and provocation to debate rather than as an attempt at ideological incorporation.

★

The science of textual scholarship as applied to early modern drama has seen considerable change in recent years: contemporary scholarly editions now aim to acknowledge these plays as dramatic scripts as well as written texts, and to take into account a play's theatrical history when attempting to produce an authoritative text. Most scholarship remains none the less committed to discovering or inferring the author's original intentions, and to producing a text which a reincarnated Shakespeare would be able to recognise and approve.[18] In the theatre, the presence of that forbidding and ghostly mythological creature, the absent author, does not always bear with quite the same gravity on the activities of those who work on and reproduce the plays in performance. Hence in the theatre history of *The Taming of the Shrew* we can witness the

[29]

emergence, in contradistinction to the priorities of scholarship, of a bold opportunism in the amalgamation of 'good' and 'bad' texts.

Anyone present at a performance of 'Shakespeare's' *The Taming of the Shrew* in Britain at any time since 1913, is quite likely to have witnessed a hybrid amalgamation of the two *Shrews*. Even the two-scene 'Induction' disappeared from the play for centuries while Garrick's *Catherine and Petruchio* and other adaptations held the stage: in 1900, Frank Benson was still producing the play with no trace of Christopher Sly. Subsequent directors such as Oscar Asche (1904), W. Bridges Adams (1933) and F. Owen Chambers (1936) restored the 'Induction', but often in a cut form. It was Martin Harvey,[19] acting under the advice and influence of William Poel, who in a 1913 production at the Prince of Wales Theatre decided to supplement the Folio text by interpolating the Christopher Sly scenes from *A Shrew*: and to develop the Sly-framework into a constitutive element of the drama. In this and many subsequent productions, Sly and his attendants were kept on stage, where they functioned as a surrogate audience: in accordance with the Lord's directions, the actors involved in the *Shrew* narrative constantly referred and deferred to them as the privileged audience of their presentation. Directors would give Sly lines which belong in the Folio text to other characters: e.g. Tranio's observation (1.1.169) 'That wench is stark mad, or wonderful froward' became, in Theodore Komisarjevsky's 1939 Stratford production, a spectator's observation from outside the dramatic event. In the same production, Sly made several abortive attempts to intervene in the action in the manner of Beaumont's intrusive grocer in *The Knight of the Burning Pestle*: at several points he tried to join the actors in the *Shrew* narrative, and had to be forcibly restrained by the page.

Since Martin Harvey's pioneering production, the Christopher Sly framework has been embraced by the modern theatre with particular enthusiasm: to such an extent that it became commonplace to augment the Folio text with the Slie interventions and epilogue preserved in the 1594 Quarto text. While in the fields of scholarship and criticism *A Shrew* was systematically distanced from the Folio text by the 'Bad Quarto' theory, the approach of theatrical practitioners was prepared to acknowledge an incompleteness, an insufficiency in the authorised Shakespeare text, by adding elements of a text generally regarded as inadequate and self-evidently un-Shakespearean, incorporated to satisfy the requirements of theatrical practice.

In 1960, John Barton directed *The Taming of the Shrew* for the newly formed Royal Shakespeare Company (see illustrations on pages 20 and 27), producing an amalgamation of the 1594 and 1623 texts. The prompt-book shows a text of the Folio play (Temple edition), redivided into fourteen scenes, with additional typed passages from *A Shrew* pasted in.[20] Barton thus chose to employ the complete Slie-frame, and to foreground the metadramatic character of the play-within-a-play format, with the *Shrew* action presented by strolling players to an on-stage surrogate audience of Slie and his attendants. When the travelling players went into the Lord, they appeared pushing their cart and carrying bundles (cp. the S.D. '*Enter two of the players with packs at their backs, and a boy*'); they engaged with the Lord in professional negotiations about the projected performance and required properties; and they included among their number a prompter, whose constant attempts to follow his script functioned to promote both comedy and a metadramatic awareness. This insistent foregrounding of the players as actors was sustained throughout the production: the permanent revolving set incorporated along with interior and exterior locations an inner 'greenroom', in which the actors could be seen rehearsing, changing costumes, drinking and playing cards.

Furthermore, Barton developed the function of Slie as a foregrounded spectator. Slie observed the play from various points of vantage on the set, a bench, a gallery, a staircase. As the set revolved he and the Lord (masquerading as the servant 'Sim' from *A Shrew*) were obliged to scramble over a staircase to keep tabs on the action. The prompt-book contains cues for Slie's reactions to the events played out before him: thus the Lord's reference to 'my trusty servant, well-approved in all' is accompanied by a stage direction '*Sly applauds*'; and Lucentio's announcement that he intends to pursue 'a course of learning and ingenious studies' receives the response '*Sly reacts with distaste*'. The performers of the play within the play were directed to display awareness of Slie as spectator – thus stage directions such as '*actors bow to Sly*' appear

[31]

frequently; and on occasions Slie could even make contact with the actors – '*Sly stops Grumio, who turns to him*'. As Vincentio was about to be unjustly imprisoned, Slie ran on to the set and stopped the action completely: 'I say wele have no sending to prison'. The actors stumbled, lost their cues and had to be started off again by the offices of the prompter.

Overall Barton's use of the Slie-frame seems to have enhanced the innocuous playfulness of the production. The frame was used very differently in a production directed, perhaps significantly, by a woman, Di Trevis. This was a Royal Shakespeare Company touring production of 1985, toured in tandem with Brecht's *Happy End*.[21] The juxtaposition was clearly not fortuitous, since the Shakespearean production was itself very Brechtian. The travelling players who enact the *Shrew*-play were foregrounded as a group of nineteenth-century actors, evidently poor and oppressed: the opening scene showed the actress who was to play Katherina pulling a cart in the style of Mother Courage. Not only was Christopher Slie kept on stage throughout as a constant choric presence, but the production maintained a constant awareness of the actors as players performing. Slie functioned consistently as an on-stage observer or surrogate audience of the players' performance; his reactions provided the actual audience with a criterion for measuring and testing their own. It was never entirely possible to forget that the play was clearly being performed by the players. Slie was foregrounded as a desperately poor and hopeless man, a victim of the Lord's capricious pranks, pathetically persuaded that he possesses power and riches. This framing effect enabled the audience both to estrange and distance the play's events, and to consider them in terms of the realities of poverty and power.

Slie himself appears to have been foregrounded more consistently and given more vigorous powers of intervention than in Barton's production. The beggar's attempted interruption of the play when Lucentio is threatened with prison was again played as a decisive disruption of the proceedings, but not merely as a comic ploy, and with a clearer crystallisation of the metadramatic dimension. Slie had evidently himself been 'inside'. The beggar's intervention threw the 'inner play' into relief, and fractured its illusions, reminding the audience unmistakably that they were watching a play. But they were also reminded of Slie's impoverished, vagrant and semi-criminal status. Slie himself is revealed as entirely under the sway of theatrical illusion: 'his involvement in the fiction of his role makes him believe in his ability to affect the fictitious events being enacted before him; but his power is as illusory as the play he watches, and as his privileged status'.[22]

These complementary emphases on fictiveness and on poverty brought a very different focus to the play's denouement. Where Barton's production resolved into reconciliation and harmony, this interpretation sustained the full implications of its metadramatic structure to the end. The taming story proceeded and ended conventionally enough, with Katherina and Petruchio achieving reconciliation and understanding. The play within a play ended with a wedding; the players took their bows and disappeared. The fiction of the taming plot was over, its illusions established. Under the sway of this sentimental romance, Slie approached his 'lady', evidently believing in the possibility of mutual affection. In a startling denouement, the page threw off his wig and ran away, with a mocking laugh. The realisation that Slie had been less a spectator than an actor in the performance was compounded by the Lord's contemptuously throwing money at his feet. The surrogate spectator is thus left bewildered and lost, unable to integrate or understand his experience of the pleasures of fiction. The actress who had played Katherina then re-entered, holding a baby and looking again downtrodden and burdened. The reconciliation by taming was revealed as a pleasant but groundless pretence, played to delude Sly and satisfy the Lord's caprice. Where Barton's production closed with a triumphant celebration of comic harmony and sentimental romance, Di Trevis' production closed – in a very Brechtian moment – with Sly offering the poor actress a share of the Lord's bounty. The poor man and the poor woman have both been victimised: and in a mutual recognition of that they find both a shared experience and a common cause.

These examples, constituting as they do the nearest thing we have to a 'stage history' of *The Taming of a Shrew*, represent of course a kind of theatrical conflation, more radical certainly than the textual conflating of modern editors, but still producing a pastiche of variant texts. One of the aspirations underlying the provision of this edition is that a genuine stage history of the more 'original' text might now become possible.

NOTES AND REFERENCES

1. The various scholarly theories attempting to explain the provenance of *The Taming of a Shrew*, and the nature of its relationship with the Folio play, can be summarised as follows:

    (i) That *The Taming of a Shrew* was written prior to *The Taming of the Shrew*, by another dramatist or dramatists, and that it was used by Shakespeare as a principal source. Earlier scholars examining *A Shrew* regarded it as a source play: for example, Thomas Amyot (ed.), *The Taming of a Shrew* (London: Shakespeare Society, 1844), and F.S. Boas (ed.), *The Taming of a Shrew* (London: Chatto & Windus, 1908). The same view was expressed by R. Warwick Bond in the Arden Shakespeare edition of *The Taming of the Shrew* (London: Methuen, 1904); by E.K. Chambers, *William Shakespeare*, vol. 1 (Oxford: Clarendon Press, 1930), pp. 322–8; and by J.W. Schroeder, *Journal of English and Germanic Philology* (1958), pp. 431–6.

    (ii) That both *The Taming of a Shrew* and *The Taming of the Shrew* derive from a third, older, unknown and lost play. The postulation of an 'Ur-Shrew' also dates back to the nineteenth century: its principal modern supporters are R.A. Houk and G.I. Duthie (see below, note 5); and W.W. Greg, *The Shakespeare First Folio* (Oxford: Clarendon Press, 1955), pp. 210–18.

    (iii) That *The Taming of a Shrew* is a 'memorial reconstruction' of *The Taming of the Shrew*, made by actors or spectators pirating Shakespeare's play for unauthorised publication. The 'Bad Quarto' theory was proposed by Peter Alexander in the *Times Literary Supplement* (16 September 1926), and 'The Original Ending of *The Taming of the Shrew*', *Shakespeare Quarterly*, 20:2 (Spring 1969), pp. 111–16, and supported by J. Dover Wilson (ed.), *The Taming of the Shrew*, New Cambridge Shakespeare (Cambridge: Cambridge University Press, 1928). Richard Hosley (see note 9 below) further developed the theory, and most modern editors have accepted this view: see for example G.R. Hibbard (ed.), *The Taming of the Shrew*, New Penguin Shakespeare (Harmondsworth: Penguin, 1968), and the editors listed in the following notes 2–4.

[34]

2. H.J. Oliver (ed.), *The Taming of the Shrew*, Oxford Shakespeare, (Oxford: Oxford University Press, 1984), pp. 13–29.

3. Brian Morris (ed.), *The Taming of the Shrew*, Arden Shakespeare (London: Methuen, 1981), pp. 12–50.

4. Ann Thompson (ed.), *The Taming of the Shrew*, New Cambridge Shakespeare (Cambridge: Cambridge University Press, 1984), pp. 155–74.

5. Samuel Hickson, 'Marlowe and the old *Taming of a Shrew*', *Notes and Queries*, 22 (1850), pp. 194, 226–7, 345–7; G.I. Duthie, '*The Taming of the Shrew* and *The Taming of a Shrew*', *Review of English Studies*, 19 (1943), pp. 337–56; R.A. Houk, 'The Evolution of *The Taming of the Shrew*', *PMLA*, 57 (1942), pp. 1009–38.

6. Morris (1981), p. 17.

7. See John Heminge and Henrie Condell, 'To the Great Variety of Readers', in Charlton Hinman (ed.), *The Norton Facsimile: the First Folio of Shakespeare* (London and New York: Paul Hamlyn, 1968), p. 7.

8. Stephen Urkowitz, 'Good News about Bad Quartos', in Maurice Charney (ed.), *'Bad' Shakespeare: Revaluations of the Shakespeare Canon* (London and Toronto: Associated University Presses, 1988), p. 204.

9. Richard Hosley, 'Sources and Analogues of *The Taming of the Shrew*', *Huntington Library Quarterly*, 27 (1964).

10. Although Slie (spelt 'Slie' in Q, 'Sly' or 'Slie' in F) is referred to in the Folio text, both on initial entry and in all speech-headings, as 'Beggar', virtually all modern editors take him at his own word and promote him in their 'Dramatis Personae' to 'tinker' (e.g. Arden, New Penguin, New Cambridge). The Oxford edition (Oliver, 1984) gives him a more comprehensive c.v. with 'drunken tinker and beggar'. Wells and Taylor (Oxford Complete Works) admit him 'drunkard and beggar', but still with all other editors alter his speech-headings from 'Beg.' to 'Sly' (and to 'Slie' in their old spelling edition). The substitution of an original emphasis on public identity and social function for a modern emphasis on personality and the individual subject (whether the focus is on a character or the character's putative creator) is a clear instance of modern editors imposing anachronistic values on an early modern text (though the systematic effacement from social obtrusion of beggars was an aspiration of the state in Elizabethan times as much as it is today).

11. See the *Shakespearean Originals* edition of the first Quarto of *Hamlet* (Hemel Hempstead: Harvester Wheatsheaf, 1992), p. 66.

12. Morris (1981), p. 37.

13. '*Faustus*: Now that the gloomy shadow of the night, / Longing to view Orion's drizzling look, / Leaps from th'antarctic world unto the

[35]

sky / And dims the welkin with her pitchy breath, / Faustus, begin thine incantations . . .' Quoted from John D. Jump (ed.), *Dr Faustus* (Manchester: Manchester University Press, 1962), p. 18.

14. H.J. Oliver (1984), p. 19.
15. For an extensive discussion of the 'scold's bridle', see Lynda E. Boose, 'Scolding Brides and Bridling Scolds: Taming the Woman's Unruly Member', *Shakespeare Quarterly*, 42:2 (Summer 1991), pp. 194–213.
16. Leah Marcus, 'Levelling Shakespeare', *Shakespeare Quarterly*, 42:2 (Summer 1991), p. 172.
17. James Worsdale, *A Cure for a Scold* (London: L. Gilliver, 1735); quoted from facsimile edition (London: Cornmarket Press, 1969), p. 60.
18. This includes the strongly theatre-inflected Oxford edition of Stanley Wells and Gary Taylor; see Margareta de Grazia, *Shakespeare Verbatim* (Oxford: Oxford University Press, 1991), p. 24n.
19. See Tori Haring-Smith, *From Farce to Metadrama: a stage history of 'The Taming of the Shrew'* (London: Greenwood Press, 1985), pp. 98–103.
20. Prompt-book for the Royal Shakespeare Company 1960 production of *The Taming of the Shrew*, dir. John Barton, held in the Shakespeare Centre Library, Stratford-upon-Avon.
21. Royal Shakespeare Company touring production of *The Taming of the Shrew*, 1985, dir. Di Trevis. Records in Shakespeare Centre Library, Stratford-upon-Avon.
22. Geraldine Cousin, 'The touring of the shrew', *New Theatre Quarterly*, 2:7 (August, 1986), p. 280.

Select Bibliography

Boose, Lynda E., 'Scolding brides and bridling scolds: Taming the woman's unruly member', *Shakespeare Quarterly*, 42:2 (Summer 1991), pp. 194–213.

Cloud, Random [Randall McCleod], 'The marriage of good and bad quartos', *Shakespeare Quarterly*, 33:4 (1982), pp. 421–30.

Cousin, Geraldine, 'The touring of the shrew', *New Theatre Quarterly*, 2:7 (August 1986), pp. 275–81.

Duthie, G.I., '*The Taming of the Shrew* and *The Taming of a Shrew*', *Review of English Studies*, 19 (1943), pp. 337–56.

Grazia, Margareta de, 'The essential Shakespeare and the material book', *Textual Practice*, 2:i (1988), pp. 69–85.

Grazia, Margareta de, *Shakespeare Verbatim* (Oxford: Oxford University Press, 1991).

Haring-Smith, Tori, *From Farce to Metadrama: A stage history of 'The Taming of the Shrew'* (London: Greenwood Press, 1985).

Hibbard, G.R., (ed.), *The Taming of the Shrew*, New Penguin Shakespeare (Harmondsworth: Penguin, 1968).

Ioppolo, Grace, *Revising Shakespeare* (Cambridge, Mass.: Harvard University Press, 1991).

Marcus, Leah, 'Levelling Shakespeare: Local customs and local texts', *Shakespeare Quarterly*, 42:ii (1991), pp. 168–78.

Morris, Brian (ed.), *The Taming of the Shrew*, Arden Shakespeare (London: Methuen, 1981).

Oliver, H.J., (ed.), *The Taming of the Shrew* (Oxford: Oxford University Press, 1984).

Orgel, Stephen, 'The authentic Shakespeare', *Representations*, 21 (Winter 1988), pp. 1–26.

Parker, Brian, 'Bowers of bliss: Deconflation in the Shakespeare canon', *New Theatre Quarterly*, 7:xxv (1991), pp. 357–61.

Small, Ian and Marcus Walsh (eds), *The Theory and Practice of Text-editing* (Cambridge: Cambridge University Press, 1991).

[37]

Select Bibliography

Thompson, Ann (ed.), *The Taming of the Shrew*, New Cambridge Shakespeare (Cambridge: Cambridge University Press, 1984).

Urkowitz, Stephen, 'Good news about bad quartos', in Maurice Charney (ed.), *Bad Shakespeare: Revaluation of the Shakespeare Canon* (London and Toronto: Associated University Presses, 1988).

Wells, Stanley, 'Theatricalizing Shakespeare's texts', *New Theatre Quarterly*, 7:xxvi (1991), pp. 184–6.

Wells, Stanley and Gary Taylor (eds), *William Shakespeare: The complete works*, and *William Shakespeare: The complete works, original-spelling edition* (Oxford: Oxford University Press, 1986).

Wells, Stanley and Gary Taylor, *William Shakespeare: A textual companion*, (Oxford: Oxford University Press, 1987).

Worsdale, James, *A Cure for a Scold* (London: L. Gilliver, 1735); facsimile edition (London: Cornmarket Press, 1969).

Textual History

O N 2 May 1594 a play with the title 'A plesant conceyted historie called the Tamynge of a Shrowe' was entered in the Stationer's register to Peter Short. In the same year appeared the first edition of *The Taming of a Shrew*, in a quarto text with the title-page inscription:

A
Pleasant Conceited
Historie, called The taming
of a Shrew.

As it was sundry times acted by the
Right honorable the Earle of
Pembrook his servants

Printed at London by Peter Short and
are to be sold by Cutbert Burbie, at his
shop at the Royall Exchange.
1594.

Only one copy of this edition survives, now in the Huntington Library, San Marino, California. A second edition was printed in 1596, and a third in 1607.

J. Nichols included the play, printed from the 3rd edition of 1607, in his *Six Old Plays* (1779); and in 1844 Thomas Amyot published an edition for the Shakespeare Society, using the 1596 and 1607 texts of the original. A facsimile reproduction of the 1594 text was made in 1886 by Charles Praetorius. The present text of *The Taming of a Shrew* has been derived from Praetorius' facsimile, as has the facsimile extract on pages 103–6 of this volume.

Modernised texts of the play have been prepared by F.S. Boas (London: Chatto & Windus, 1908), and by Geoffrey Bullough for his *Narrative and Dramatic Sources of Shakespeare*, vol. 1 (London: Routledge & Kegan Paul, 1966).

A

Pleaſant Conceited

Hiſtorie, called The taming
of a Shrew.

As it was ſundry times acted by the
Right honorable the Earle of
Pembrook his ſeruants.

Printed at London by Peter Short and
are to be ſold by Cutbert Burbie, at his
ſhop at the Royall Exchange.
1594.

A PLEASANT CONCEITED HISTORIE,
CALLED
The Taming of a Shrew

Enter a Tapster, beating out of his doores
Slie Droonken.

Tapster. You whorson droonken slave, you had best be
gone,
And empty your droonken panch some where else
For in this house thou shalt not rest to night.

Exit Tapster.

Slie. Tilly vally, by crisee Tapster Ile fese you anon.
Fils the tother pot and alls paid for, looke you
I doo drinke it of mine own Instegation, *Omne Bene*
Heere Ile lie a while, why Tapster I say,
Fils a fresh cushen heere.
Heigh ho, heers good warme lying.

He fals asleepe.

Enter a Noble man and his men
from hunting.

Lord. Now that the gloomie shaddow of the night,
Longing to view Orions drisling lookes,
Leapes from th'antarticke World unto the skie
And dims the Welkin with her pitchie breath,
And darkesome night oreshades the christall heavens,

[43]

Here breake we off our hunting for to night,
Cupple uppe the hounds and let us hie us home,
And bid the huntsman see them meated well,
For they have all deserv'd it well to daie,
But soft, what sleepie fellow is this lies heere?
Or is he dead, see one what he dooth lacke?
 Servingman. My lord, tis nothing but a drunken sleepe,
His head is too heavie for his bodie,
And he hath drunke so much that he can go no furder.
 Lord. Fie, how the slavish villaine stinkes of drinke.
Ho, sirha arise. What so sound asleepe?
Go take him uppe and beare him to my house,
And beare him easilie for feare he wake,
And in my fairest chamber make a fire,
And set a sumptuous banquet on the boord,
And put my richest garmentes on his backe,
Then set him at the Table in a chaire:
When that is doone against he shall awake,
Let heavenlie musicke play about him still,
Go two of you awaie and beare him hence,
And then Ile tell you what I have devisde,
But see in any case you wake him not.

Exeunt two with *Slie.*

Now take my cloake and give me one of yours,
Al fellowes now, and see you take me so,
For we will waite upon this droonken man,
To see his countnance when he dooth awake
And finde himselfe clothed in such attire,
With heavenlie musicke sounding in his eares,
And such a banquet set before his eies,
The fellow sure will thinke he is in heaven,
But we will be about him when he wakes,
And see you call him Lord, at everie word,
And offer thou him his horse to ride abroad,
And thou his hawkes and houndes to hunt the deere,
And I will aske what sutes he meanes to weare,

And what so ere he saith see you doo not laugh,
But still perswade him that he is a Lord.

Enter one.

Mes. And it please your honour your plaiers be com
And doo attend your honours pleasure here.
Lord. The fittest time they could have chosen out,
Bid one or two of them come hither straight,
Now will I fit my selfe accordinglie,
For they shall play to him when he awakes.

Enter two of the players with packs at their
backs, and a boy.

Now sirs, what store of plaies have you?
San. Marrie my lord you maie have a Tragicall
Or a comoditie, or what you will.
The other. A Comedie thou shouldst say, souns
thout shame us all.
Lord. And whats the name of your Comedie?
San. Marrie my lord tis calde The taming of a shrew:
Tis a good lesson for us my lord, for us that are maried men.
Lord. The taming of a shrew, thats excellent sure,
Go see that you make you readie straight,
For you must play before a lord to night,
Say you are his men and I your fellow,
Hees something foolish, but what so ere he saies,
See that you be not dasht out of countenance.
And sirha go you make you ready straight,
And dresse your selfe like some lovelie ladie,
And when I call see that you come to me,
For I will say to him thou art his wife,
Dallie with him and hug him in thine armes,
And if he desire to goe to bed with thee,
Then faine some scuse and say thou wilt anon.
Be gone, I say, and see thou doost it well.
Boy. Feare not my Lord, Ile dandell him well enough
And make him thinke I love him mightilie.   *Ex.* boy.

[45]

The taming of a Shrew

Lord. Now sirs go you and make you ready to,
For you must play assoone as he dooth wake.
  San. O brave, sirha Tom, we must play before
A foolish Lord, come lets go make us ready,
Go get a dishclout to make cleane your shooes,
And Ile speake for the properties, My Lord, we must
Have a shoulder of mutton for a propertie,
And a little vinegre to make our Divell rore.
  Lord. Very well: sirha see that they want nothing.

                                        Exeunt omnes.

   Enter two with a table and a banquet on it, and two
       other, with *Slie* asleepe in a chaire, richlie
           apparelled, & the musick plaieng.

One. So: sirha now go call my Lord,
And tel him that all things is ready as he wild it.
  Another. Set thou some wine upon the boord
And then Ile go fetch my Lord presentlie.   *Exit.*

            Enter the Lord and his men.

Lord. How now, what is all thinges readie?
One. I my Lord.
Lord. Then sound the musick, and Ile wake him straight,
And see you doo as earst I gave in charge.
My lord, My lord, he sleepes soundlie: My lord.
  Slie. Tapster, gis a little small ale. Heigh ho,
Lord. Heers wine my lord, the purest of the grape.
Slie. For which Lord?
Lord. For your honour my Lord.
Slie. Who I, am I a Lord? Jesus what fine apparell
have I got.
  Lord. More richer farre your honour hath to weare,
And if it please you I will fetch them straight.
  Wil. And if your honour please to ride abroad,
Ile fetch you lusty steedes more swift of pace
Then winged *Pegasus* in all his pride,

                    [46]

That ran so swiftlie over the *Persian* plaines.

Tom. And if your honour please to hunt the deere,
Your hounds stands readie cuppeld at the doore,
Who in running will oretake the Row,
And make the long breathde Tygre broken winded.

Slie. By the masse I thinke I am a Lord indeed,
Whats thy name?

Lord. *Simon* and it please your honour.

Slie. *Simon*, thats as much to say *Simion or Simon*
Put foorth thy hand and fill the pot.
Give me thy hand, *Sim.* am I a lord indeed?

Lord. I my gratious Lord, and your lovelie ladie
Long time hath moorned for your absence heere,
And now with joy behold where she dooth come
To gratulate your honours safe returne.

Enter the boy in Womans attire.

Slie. Sim. Is this she?

Lord. I my Lord.

Slie. Masse tis a prettie wench, whats her name?

Boy. Oh that my lovelie Lord would once vouchsafe
To looke on me, and leave these frantike fits,
Or were I now but halfe so eloquent,
To paint in words what ile performe in deedes,
I know your honour then would pittie me.

Slie. Harke you mistresse, wil you eat a peece of bread,
Come sit downe on my knee, *Sim* drinke to hir *Sim*,
For she and I will go to bed anon.

Lord. May it please you, your honors plaiers be come
To offer your honour a plaie.

Slie. A plaie *Sim*, O brave, be they my plaiers?

Lord. I my Lord.

Slie. Is there not a foole in the plaie?

Lord. Yes my lord.

Slie. When wil they plaie *Sim*?

Lord. Even when it please your honor, they be readie.

Boy. My lord Ile go bid them begin their plaie.

[47]

Slie. Doo, but looke that you come againe.
Boy. I warrant you my lord, I wil not leave you thus.

Exit boy.

Slie. Come *Sim*, where be the plaiers? *Sim* stand by
Me and weele flout the plaiers out of their cotes.
Lord. Ile cal them my lord. Hoe where are you there?

Sound Trumpets.

Enter two yoong Gentlemen, and a man
and a boie.

Pol. Welcome to *Athens* my beloved friend,
To *Platoes* schooles and *Aristotles* walkes,
Welcome from *Cestus* famous for the love
Of good *Leander* and his Tragedie,
For whom the *Helespont* weepes brinish teares,
The greatest griefe is I cannot as I would
Give entertainment to my deerest friend.
Aurel. Thankes noble *Polidor* my second selfe,
The faithfull love which I have found in thee
Hath made me leave my fathers princelie court,
The Duke of *Cestus* thrise renowmed seate,
To come to *Athens* thus to find thee out,
Which since I have so happilie attaind,
My fortune now I doo account as great
As earst did *Casar* when he conquered most,
But tell me noble friend where shal we lodge,
For I am unacquainted in this place.
Poli. My Lord if you vouchsafe of schollers fare,
My house, my selfe, and all is yours to use,
You and your men shall staie and lodge with me.
Aurel. With all my hart, I will requite thy love.

Enter *Simon, Alphonsus*, and his
three daughters.

But staie; what dames are these so bright of hew
Whose eies are brighter then the lampes of heaven,

[48]

Fairer then rocks of pearle and pretious stone,
More lovelie farre then is the morning sunne,
When first she opes hir orientall gates.

Alfon. Daughters be gone, and hie you to the church,
And I will hie me downe unto the key,
To see what Marchandise is come a shore.

Ex. Omnes.

Pol. Why how now my Lord, what in a dumpe,
To see these damsels passe away so soone?

Aurel. Trust me my friend I must confesse to thee,
I tooke so much delight in these faire dames,
As I doo wish they had not gone so soone,
But if thou canst, resolve me what they be,
And what old man it was that went with them,
For I doo long to see them once againe.

Pol. I cannot blame your honor good my lord,
For they are both lovely, wise, faire and yong,
And one of them the yoongest of the three
I long have lov'd (sweet friend) and she lov'd me,
But never yet we could not find a meanes
How we might compasse our desired joyes.

Aurel. Why, is not her father willing to the match?

Pol. Yes trust me, but he hath solemnlie sworne,
His eldest daughter first shall be espowsde,
Before he grauntes his yoongest leave to love,
And therefore he that meanes to get their loves,
Must first provide for her if he will speed,
And he that hath her shall be fettred so,
As good be wedded to the divell himselfe,
For such a skould as she did never live,
And till that she be sped none else can speed,
Which makes me thinke that all my labours lost,
And whosoere can get hir firme good will,
A large dowrie he shall be sure to have,
For her father is a man of mightie wealth,
And an ancient Cittizen of the towne,
And that was he that went along with them.

[49]

Aurel. But he shall keepe hir still by my advise,
And yet I needs must love his second daughter
The image of honor and Nobilitie,
In whose sweet person is comprisde the somme
Of natures skill and heavenlie majestie.

   Pol. I like your choise, and glad you chose not mine,
Then if you like to follow on your love,
We must devise a meanes and find some one
That will attempt to wed this devilish skould,
And I doo know the man. Come hither boy,
Go your waies sirha to *Ferandoes* house,
Desire him take the paines to come to me,
For I must speake with him immediatlie.

   Boy. I will sir, and fetch him presentlie.

   Pol. A man I thinke will fit hir humor right,
As blunt in speech as she is sharpe of toong,
And he I thinke will match hir everie waie,
And yet he is a man of wealth sufficient,
And for his person worth as good as she,
And if he compasse hir to be his wife,
Then may we freelie visite both our loves.

   Aurel. O might I see the center of my soule
Whose sacred beautie hath inchanted me,
More faire than was the Grecian *Helena*
For whose sweet sake so many princes dide,
That came with thousand shippes to *Tenedos*,
But when we come unto hir fathers house,
Tell him I am a Marchants sonne of *Cestus*,
That comes for traffike unto *Athens* heere,
And heere sirha I will change with you for once,
And now be thou the Duke of *Cestus* sonne,
Revell and spend as if thou wert my selfe,
For I will court my love in this disguise.

   Val. My lord, how if the Duke your father should
By some meanes come to *Athens* for to see
How you doo profit in the e publike schooles,
And find me clothed thus in your attire,

How would he take it then thinke you my lord?
Aurel. Tush feare not *Valeria* let me alone,
But staie, heere comes some other companie.

Enter *Ferando* and his man *Saunders*
with a blew coat.

Pol. Here comes the man that I did tel you of.
Feran. Good morrow gentlemen to all at once.
How now *Polidor*, what man still in love?
Ever wooing and canst thou never speed,
God send me better luck when I shall woo.
San. I warrant you maister and you take my councell.
Feran. Why sirha, are you so cunning?
San. Who I, twere better for you by five marke
And you could tel how to doo it as well as I.
Pol. I would thy maister once were in the vaine,
To trie himselfe how he could woe a wench.
Feran. Faith I am even now a going.
San. I faith sir, my maisters going to this geere now.
Pol. Whither in faith *Ferando*, tell me true.
Feran. To bonie *Kate*, the patientst wench alive
The divel himselfe dares scarce venter to woo her,
Signior *Alfonsos* eldest daughter,
And he hath promisde me six thousand crownes
If I can win her once to be my wife,
And she and I must woo with skoulding sure,
And I will hold her toot till she be wearie,
Or else Ile make her yeeld to graunt me love.
Pol. How like you this *Aurelius*, I thinke he knew
Our mindes before we sent to him,
But tell me, when doo you meane to speake with her?
Feran. Faith presentlie, doo you but stand aside,
And I will make her father bring hir hither,
And she, and I, and he, will talke alone.
Pol. With al our heartes, Come *Aurelius*
Let us be gone and leave him heere alone.   *Exit.*
Feran. Ho Signiour *Alfonso*, whose within there?

[51]

Alfon. Signiour *Ferando* your welcome hartilie,
You are a stranger sir unto my house.
Harke you sir, looke what I did promise you
Ile performe, if you get my daughters love.
  Feran. Then when I have talkt a word or two with hir,
Doo you step in and give her hand to me,
And tell her when the marriage daie shal be,
For I doo know she would be married faine,
And when our nuptiall rites be once performde
Let me alone to tame hir well enough,
Now call her foorth that I may speake with hir.

Enter Kate.

Alfon. Ha *Kate*, Come hither wench & list to me,
Use this gentleman friendlie as thou canst.
  Feran. Twentie good morrowes to my lovely *Kate*.
  Kate. You jest I am sure, is she yours alreadie?
  Feran. I tell thee *Kate* I know thou lov'st me well.
  Kate. The devill you doo, who told you so?
  Feran. My mind sweet *Kate* doth say I am the man,
Must wed, and bed, and marrie bonnie *Kate*.
  Kate. Was ever seene so grose an asse as this?
  Feran. I, to stand so long and never get a kisse.
  Kate. Hands off I say, and get you from this place;
Or I will set my ten commandments in your face.
  Feran. I prethe doo kate; they say thou art a shrew,
And I like thee the better for I would have thee so.
  Kate. Let go my hand, for feare it reach your eare.
  Feran. No kate, this hand is mine and I thy love.
  Kate. In faith sir no the woodcock wants his taile.
  Feran. But yet his bil wil serve, if the other faile.
  Alfon. How now *Ferando*, what saies my daughter?
  Feran. Shees willing sir and loves me as hir life.
  Kate. Tis for your skin then, but not to be your wife.
  Alfon. Come hither *Kate* and let me give thy hand
To him that I have chosen for thy love,
And thou to morrow shalt be wed to him.

[52]

The taming of a Shrew

Kate. Why father, what do you meane to do with me,
To give me thus unto this brainsick man,
That in his mood cares not to murder me?

She turnes aside and speakes.

But yet I will consent and marrie him,
For I methinkes have livde too long a maid,
And match him to, or else his manhoods good.
    Alfon. Give me thy hand *Ferando* loves thee wel,
And will with wealth and ease maintaine thy state.
Here *Ferando* take her for thy wife,
And sunday next shall be your wedding day.
    Feran. Why so, did I not tell thee I should be the man
Father, I leave my lovelie *Kate* with you,
Provide your selves against our mariage daie,
For I must hie me to my countrie house
In hast, to see provision may be made,
To entertaine my *Kate* when she dooth come.
    Alfon. Doo so, come *Kate*, why doost thou looke
So sad, be merrie wench thy wedding daies at hand.
Sonne fare you well, and see you keepe your promise.

Exit Alfonso and *Kate.*

Feran. So, all thus farre goes well. Ho *Saunder.*

Enter *Saunder* laughing.

San. Sander, I faith your a beast, I crie God hartilie
Mercie, my harts readie to run out of my bellie with
Laughing, I stood behind the doore all this while,
And heard what you said to hir.
    Feran. Why didst thou think that I did not speake wel
to hir?
    San. You spoke like an asse to her, Ile tel you what,
And I had been there to have woode hir, and had this
Cloke on that you have, chud have had her before she
Had gone a foot furder, and you talke of Woodcocks

[53]

with her, and I cannot tell you what.

Feran. Wel sirha, & yet thou seest I have got her for all this.

San. I marry twas more by hap than any good cunning
I hope sheele make you one of the head men of the
parish shortly.

Feran. Wel sirha leave your jesting and go to *Polidors*
house,
The yong gentleman that was here with me,
And tell him the circumstance of all thou knowst,
Tell him on sunday next we must be married,
And if he aske thee whither I am gone,
Tell him into the countrie to my house,
And upon sundaie Ile be heere againe.   *Ex Ferando,*

San. I warrant you Maister feare not me
For dooing of my businesse.
Now hang him that has not a liverie cote
To slash it out and swash it out amongst the proudest
On them. Why looke you now Ile scarce put up
Plaine *Saunder* now at any of their handes, for and any
Bodie have any thing to doo with my maister, straight
They come crouching upon me, I beseech you good M.
Saunder speake a good word for me, and then I am so
Stout and takes it upon me, & stands upon my pantoflles
To them out of all crie, why I have a life like a giant
Now, but that my maister hath such a pestilent mind
To a woman now a late, and I have a prettie wench
To my sister, and I had thought to have preferd my
Maister to her, and that would have beene a good
Deale in my waie but that hees sped alreadie.

Enter *Polidors* boie

Boy. Friend, well met.

San. Souns, friend well met. I hold my life he sees
Not my maisters liverie coat,
Plaine friend hop of my thum, kno you who we are.

Boy. Trust me sir it is the use where I was borne,
To salute men after this manner, yet notwithstanding

If you be angrie with me for calling of you friend,
I am the more sorie for it, hoping the stile
Of a foole will make you amends for all.
    San. The slave is sorie for his fault, now we cannot be
Angrie, wel whats the matter that you would do with us.
    Boy. Marry sir, I heare you pertain to signior *Ferando.*
    San. I and thou beest not blind thou maist see,
Ecce signum, heere.
    Boy. Shall I intreat you to doo me a message to your
Maister?
    San. I, it may be, & you tel us from whence you com.
    Boy. Marrie sir I serve yong *Polidor* your maisters friend.
    San. Do you serve him, and whats your name?
    Boy. My name sirha, I tell thee sirha is cald Catapie.
    San. Cake and pie, O my teeth waters to have a peece
of thee.
    Boy. Why slave wouldst thou eate me?
    San. Eat thee, who would not eate Cake and pie?
    Boy. Why villaine my name is Catapie,
But wilt thou tell me where thy maister is.
    San. Nay thou must first tell me where thy maister is,
For I have good newes for him, I can tell thee.
    Boy. Why see where he comes.

Enter *Polidor, Aurelius* and *Valeria.*

    Pol. Come sweet *Aurelius* my faithfull friend,
Now will we go to see those lovelie dames
Richer in beawtie then the orient pearle,
Whiter then is the Alpine Christall mould,
And farre more lovelie then the terean plant,
That blushing in the aire turnes to a stone.
What *Sander*, what newes with you?
    San. Marry sir my maister sends you word
That you must come to his wedding to morrow.
    Pol. What, shall he be married then?
    San. Faith I, you thinke he standes as long about it as
you doo.

[55]

Pol. Whither is thy maister gone now?

San. Marrie hees gone to our house in the Countrie,
To make all thinges in a readinesse against my new
Mistresse comes thither, but heele come againe to morrowe.

Pol. This is suddainlie dispatcht belike.
Well, sirha boy, take *Saunder* in with you
And have him to the buttrie presentlie.

Boy. I will sir: come *Saunder*.

Exit Saunder and the Boy.

Aurel. *Valeria* as erste we did devise,
Take thou thy lute and go to *Alfonsos* house,
And say that *Polidor* sent thee thither.

Pol. I *Valeria* for he spoke to me,
To helpe him to some cunning Musition,
To teach his eldest daughter on the lute,
And thou I know will fit his turne so well
As thou shalt get great favour at his handes,
Begon *Valeria* and say I sent thee to him.

Valer. I will sir and stay your comming at *Alfonsos*
house.

Exit Valeria

Pol. Now sweete *Aurelius* by this devise
Shall we have leisure for to courte our loves,
For whilst that she is learning on the lute,
Hir sisters may take time to steele abrode,
For otherwise shele keep them both within,
And make them worke whilst she hir selfe doth play,
But come lets go unto *Alfonsos* house,
And see how *Valeria* and *Kate* agreese,
I doute his Musick skarse will please his skoller,
But stay here comes *Alfonso*.

Enter Alfonso

Alfonso. What M. *Polidor* you are well mett,

[56]

I thanke you for the man you sent to me,
A good Musition I thinke he is,
I have set my daughter and him togither,
But is this gentellman a frend of youres?
   Pol. He is, I praie you sir bid him welcome,
He's a wealthie Marchants sonne of *Cestus.*
   Alfonso. Your welcom sir and if my house aforde
You any thing that may content your mind,
I pray you sir make bold with me.
   Aurel. I thanke you sir, and if what I have got,
By marchandise or travell on the seas,
Sattins or lawnes or azure colloured silke,
Or pretious firie pointed stones of Indie,
You shall command both them my selfe and all.
   Alfon. Thanks gentle sir, *Polidor* take him in,
And bid him welcome to unto my house,
For thou I thinke must be my second sonne,
Ferando, Polidor doost thou not know
Must marry *Kate,* and to morrow is the day.
   Pol. Such newes I heard, and I came now to know.
   Alfon. *Polidor* tis true, goe let me alone,
For I must see against the bridegroome come,
That all thinges be according to his mind,
And so Ile leave you for an houre or two.   *Exit.*
   Pol. Come then *Aureleus* come in with me,
And weele go sit a while and chat with them,
And after bring them foorth to take the aire.   *Exit.*

Then Slie speakes.

   Slie. *Sim,* when will the foole come againe?
   Lord. Heele come againe my Lord anon.
   Slie. Gis some more drinke here, souns wheres
The Tapster, here *Sim* eate some of these things.
   Lord. So I doo my Lord.
   Slie. Here *Sim,* I drinke to thee.
   Lord. My Lord heere comes the plaiers againe,
   Slie. O brave, heers two fine gentlewomen.

[57]

The taming of a Shrew

Enter *Valeria* with a Lute and *Kate*
with him.

Vale. The sencelesse trees by musick have bin moov'd
And at the sound of pleasant tuned strings,
Have savage beastes hung downe their listning heads,
As though they had beene cast into a trance.
Then it may be that she whom nought can please,
With musickes sound in time may be surprisde,
Come lovely mistresse will you take your lute,
And play the lesson that I taught you last?
Kate. It is no matter whether I doo or no,
For trust me I take no great delight in it.
Vale. I would sweet mistresse that it laie in me,
To helpe you to that thing thats your delight.
Kate. In you with a pestlence, are you so kind?
Then make a night cap of your fiddles case,
To warme your head, and hide your filthie face.
Val. If that sweet mistresse were your harts content,
You should command a greater thing then that,
Although it were ten times to my disgrace.
Kate. Your so kind twere pittie you should be hang'd,
And yet methinkes the foole dooth looke asquint.
Val. Why mistresse doo you mocke me?
Kate. No, but I meane to move thee.
Val. Well, will you plaie a little?
Kate. I, give me the Lute.

She plaies.

Val. That stop was false, play it againe.
Kate. Then mend it thou, thou filthy asse.
Val. What, doo you bid me kisse your arse?
Kate. How now jack sause, your a jollie mate,
Your best be still least I crosse your pate,
And make your musicke flie about your eares,
Ile make it and your foolish coxcombe meet.

She offers to strike him with the lute.

[58]

Val. Hold mistresse, souns wil you breake my lute?
Kate. I on thy head, and if thou speake to me,
There take it up and fiddle somewhere else,

She throwes it downe.

And see you come no more into this place,
Least that I clap your fiddle on your face.   *Ex. Kate.*
Val. Souns, teach hir to play upon the lute?
The devill shal teach her first, I am glad shees gone,
For I was neare so fraid in all my life,
But that my lute should flie about mine eares,
My maister shall teach her his selfe for me,
For Ile keepe me far enough without hir reach,
For he and Polydor sent me before
To be with her and teach her on the lute,
Whilst they did court the other gentlewomen,
And heere methinkes they come togither.

Enter *Aurelius, Polidor, Emelia,*
and *Philena.*

Pol. How now *Valeria,* whears your mistresse?
Val. At the vengeance I thinke and no where else.
Aurel. Why *Valeria,* will she not learne apace?
Val. Yes berlady she has learnt too much already,
And that I had felt had I not spoke hir faire,
But she shall neare be learnt for me againe.
Aurel. Well *Valeria* go to my chamber,
And bear him companie that came to daie
From *Cestus,* where our aged father dwels.   *Ex. Valeria.*
Pol. Come faire *Emelia* my lovelie love,
Brighter then the burnisht pallace of the sunne,
The eie-sight of the glorious firmament,
In whose bright lookes sparkles the radiant fire,
Wilie *Prometheus* slilie stole from *Iove,*
Infusing breath, life, motion, soule,
To everie object striken by thine eies.
Oh faire *Emelia* I pine for thee,

[59]

And either must enjoy thy love, or die.
    Eme. Fie man, I know you will not die for love.
Ah *Polidor* thou needst not to complaine,
Eternall heaven sooner be dissolvde,
And all that pearseth Phebus silver eie,
Before such hap befall to *Polidor.*
    Pol. Thanks faire *Emelia* for these sweet words,
But what saith *Phylena* to hir friend?
    Phyle. Why I am buying marchandise of him.
    Aurel. Mistresse you shall not need to buie of me,
For when I crost the bubling Canibey,
And sailde along the Cristall Helispont,
I filde my cofers of the wealthie mines,
Where I did cause Millions of labouring Moores
To undermine the cavernes of the earth,
To seeke for strange and new found pretious stones,
And dive into the sea to gather pearle,
As faire as *Juno* offered *Priams* sonne,
And you shall take your liberall choice of all.
    Phyle. I thanke you sir and would *Phylena* might
In any curtesie requite you so,
As she with willing hart could well bestow.

Enter Alfonso.

    Alfon. How now daughters, is *Ferando* come?
    Eme. Not yet father, I wonder he staies so long.
    Alfon. And wheres your sister that she is not heere?
    Phyle. She is making of hir readie father
To goe to church and if that he were come.
    Pol. I warrant you heele not be long awaie.
    Alfon. Go daughters get you in, and bid your
Sister provide her selfe against that we doo come,
And see you goe to church along with us.

Exit Philena and Emelia.

I marvell that *Ferando* comes not away.
    Pol. His Tailor it may be hath bin too slacke,

[60]

In his apparrell which he meanes to weare,
For no question but some fantasticke sutes
He is determined to weare to day,
And richly powdered with pretious stones,
Spotted with liquid gold, thick set with pearle,
And such he meanes shall be his wedding sutes.
    Alfon. I carde not I what cost he did bestow,
In gold or silke, so he himselfe were heere,
For I had rather lose a thousand crownes,
Then that he should deceive us heere to daie,
But soft I thinke I see him come.

    Enter *Ferando* baselie attired, and a red cap on his head.

    Feran. Godmorrow father, *Polidor* well met,
You wonder I know that I have staid so long.
    Aurel. I marrie son, we were almost perswaded,
That we should scarse have had our bridegroome heere,
But say, why art thou thus basely attired?
    Feran. Thus richlie father you should have said,
For when my wife and I am married once,
Shees such a shrew, if we should once fal out,
Sheele pul my costlie sutes over mine eares,
And therefore am I thus attired awhile,
For manie thinges I tell you's in my head,
And none must know thereof but *Kate* and I,
For we shall live like lammes and Lions sure,
Nor lammes to Lions never was so tame,
If once they lie within the Lions pawes
As *Kate* to me if we were married once,
And therefore come let us to church presently,
    Pol. Fie *Ferando* not thus atired for shame,
Come to my Chamber and there sute thy selfe,
Of twentie sutes that I did never were.
    Feran. Tush *Polidor* I have as many sutes
Fantasticke made to fit my humor so
As any in Athens and as richlie wrought
As was the Massie Robe that late adornd,

[61]

The stately legate of the Persian King,
And this from them have I made choise to weare.
   Alfon. I prethie *Ferando* let me intreat
Before thou goste unto the church with us,
To put some other sute upon thy backe.
   Feran. Not for the world if I might gaine it so,
And therefore take me thus or not at all,

Enter Kate.

But soft se where my *Kate* doth come,
I must salute hir: how fares my lovely *Kate*?
What art thou readie? shall we go to church?
   Kate. Not I with one so mad, so basely tirde,
To marrie such a filthie slavish groome,
That as it seemes sometimes is from his wits,
Or else he would not thus have come to us.
   Feran. Tush *Kate* these words addes greater love in me
And makes me thinke thee fairrer then before,
Sweete *Kate* the lovelier then Dianas purple robe,
Whiter then are the snowie Apenis,
Or icie haire that groes on Boreas chin.
Father I sweare by Ibis golden beake,
More faire and Radiente is my bonie *Kate*,
Then silver Zanthus when he doth imbrace,
The ruddie Simies at Idas feete,
And care not thou swete *Kate* how I be clad,
Thou shalt have garments wrought of Median silke,
Enchast with pretious Jewells fecht from far,
By Italian Marchants that with Russian stemes,
Plous up huge forrowes in the *Terren Maine*,
And better farre my lovely *Kate* shall weare,
Then come sweet love and let us to the church
For this I sweare shall be my wedding sute.

Exeunt omn.

   Alfon. Come gentlemen go along with us,
For thus doo what we can he will be wed.   *Exit.*

[62]

The taming of a Shrew

Enter *Polidors* boy and *Sander*.

Boy. Come hither sirha boy.

San. Boy; oh disgrace to my person, souns boy
Of your face, you have many boies with such
Pickadevantes I am sure, souns would you
Not have a bloudie nose for this?

Boy. Come, come, I did but jest, where is that
Same peece of pie that I gave thee to keepe.

San. The pie? I you have more minde of your bellie
Then to go see what your maister dooes.

Boy. Tush tis no matter man I prethe give it me,
I am verie hungry I promise thee.

San. Why you may take it and the devill burst
You with it, one cannot save a bit after supper,
But you are alwaies readie to munch it up.

Boy. Why come man, we shall have good cheere
Anon at the bridehouse; for your maisters gone to
Church to be married alreadie, and thears
Such cheere as passeth.

San. O brave, I would I had eate no meat this week,
For I have never a corner left in my bellie
To put a venson pastie in, I thinke I shall burst my selfe
With eating, for Ile so cram me downe the tarts
And the marchpaines, out of all crie.

Boy. I, but how wilt thou doo now thy maisters
Married, thy mistresse is such a devill, as sheele make
Thee forget thy eating quickly, sheele beat thee so.

San. Let my maister alone with hir for that, for
Heele make hir tame wel inough ere longe I warent thee
For he's such a churle waxen now of late that and he be
Never so little angry he thums me out of all crie,
But in my mind sirra the yongest is a verie
Prettie wench, and if I thought thy maister would
Not have hir Ide have a fling at hir
My selfe, Ile see soone whether twill be a match
Or no: and it will not Ile set the matter

[63]

Hard for my selfe I warrant thee.

Boy. Sounes you slave will you be a Rivall with
My maister in his love, speake but such
Another worde and Ile cut off one of thy legges.

San. Oh, cruell judgement, nay then sirra,
My tongue shall talke no more to you, marry my
Timber shall tell the trustie message of his maister,
Even on the very forehead on thee, thou abusious
Villaine, therefore prepare thy selfe.

Boy. Come hither thou Imperfecksious slave in
Regard of thy beggery, holde thee theres
Two shillings for thee? to pay for the
Healing of thy left legge which I meane
Furiously to invade or to maime at the least.

San. O supernodicall foule? well Ile take your
two shillinges but Ile barre striking at legges.

Boy. Not I, for Ile strike any where.

San. Here here take your two shillings again
Ile see thee hangd ere Ile fight with thee,
I gat a broken shin the other day,
Tis not, whole yet and therefore Ile not fight
Come come why should we fall out?

Boy. Well sirray your faire words hath something
Alaied my Coller: I am content for this once
To put it up and be frends with thee,
But soft see where they come all from church,
Belike they be Married allredy.

> Enter *Ferando and Kate and Alfonso and Polidor
> and Emelia and Aurelius and Philema.*

Feran. Father farwell, my *Kate* and I must home,
Sirra go make ready my horse presentlie.

Alfon. Your horse! what son I hope you doo but jest,
I am sure you will not go so suddainly.

Kate. Let him go or tarry I am resolv'de to stay,
And not to travell on my wedding day.

[64]

Feran. Tut *Kate* I tell thee we must needes go home,
Villaine hast thou saddled my horse?
    San. Which horse, your curtall?
    Feran. Sounes you slave stand you prating here?
Saddell the bay gelding for your Mistris.
    Kate. Not for me: for Ile not go.
    San. The ostler will not let me have him, you owe ten
pence
For his meate, and 6 pence for stuffing my mistris saddle.
    Feran. Here villaine go pay him straight.
    San. Shall I give them another pecke of lavender.
    Feran. Out slave and bring them presently to the dore.
    Alfon. Why son I hope at least youle dine with us.
    San. I pray you maister lets stay till dinner be don.
    Feran. Sounes villaine art thou here yet?   *Ex. Sander.*
Come *Kate* our dinner is provided at home.
    Kate. But not for me, for here I meane to dine.
Ile have my will in this as well as you,
Though you in madding mood would leave your frends
Despite of you Ile tarry with them still.
    Feran. I *Kate* so thou shalt but at some other time,
When as thy sisters here shall be espousd,
Then thou and I will keepe our wedding day,
In better sort then now we can provide,
For here I promise thee before them all,
We will ere long returne to them againe,
Come *Kate* stand not on termes we will awaie,
This is my day, to morrow thou shalt rule,
And I will doo what ever thou commandes.
Gentlemen farwell, wele take our leves,
It will be late before that we come home.

        Exit Ferando and Kate.

Pol. Farwell *Ferando* since you will be gone.
    Alfon. So mad a cupple did I never see.
    Emel. They're even as well macht as I would wish.
    Phile. And yet I hardly thinke that he can tame her.

For when he has don she will do what she list.
  Aurel. Her manhood then is good I do beleeve.
  Pol. Aurelius or else I misse my marke,
Her toung will walke if she doth hold her handes,
I am in dout ere halfe a month be past
Hele curse the priest that married him so soone,
And yet it may be she will be reclaimde,
For she is verie patient grone of late.
  Alfon. God hold it that it may continue still,
I would be loth that they should disagree,
But he I hope will holde her in a while.
  Pol. Within this two daies I will ride to him,
And see how lovingly they do agree.
  Alfon. Now *Aurelius* what say you to this,
What have you sent to *Cestus* as you said,
To certifie your father of your love,
For I would gladlie he would like of it,
And if he be the man you tell to me,
I gesse he is a Marchant of great wealth.
And I have seene him oft at *Athens* here,
And for his sake assure thee thou art welcome.
  Pol. And so to me whilest *Polidor* doth live.
  Aurel. I find it so right worthie gentlemen,
And of what worth your frendship I esteme,
I leve censure of your severall thoughts,
But for requitall of your favours past,
Rests yet behind, which when occasion serves
I vow shalbe remembred to the full,
And for my fathers comming to this place,
I do expect within this weeke at most.
  Alfon. Inough *Aurelius?* but we forget
Our Marriage dinner, now the bride is gon,
Come let us se what there they left behind.   *Exit Omnes*

*Enter Sanders with two or three
serving men*

  San. Come sirs provide all thinges as fast as you can,

[66]

For my Masters hard at hand and my new Mistris
And all, and he sent me before to see all thinges redy.

Tom. Welcome home *Sander* sirra how lookes our
New Mistris they say she's a plagie shrew.

San. I and that thou shalt find I can tell thee and thou
Dost not please her well, why my Maister
Has such a doo with hir as it passeth and he's even
like a madman.

Will. Why *Sander* what dos he say.

San. Why Ile tell you what: when they should
Go to church to be maried he puts on an olde
Jerkin and a paire of canvas breeches downe to the
Small of his legge and a red cap on his head and he
Lookes as thou wilt burst thy selfe with laffing
When thou seest him: he's ene as good as a
Foole for me: and then when they should go to dinner
He made me Saddle the horse and away he came.
And nere tarried for dinner and therefore you had best
Get supper reddy against they come, for
They be hard at hand I am sure by this time.

Tom. Sounes see where they be all redy.

Enter Ferando and Kate.

Feran. Now welcome *Kate*: wher'es these villains
Here, what? not supper yet uppon the borde:
Nor table spred nor nothing don at all,
Wheres that villaine that I sent before.

San. Now, *adsum*, sir.

Feran. Come hether you villaine Ile cut your nose,
You Rogue: helpe me of with my bootes: wilt please
You to lay the cloth? sounes the villaine
Hurts my foote? pull easely I say; yet againe.

He beats them all.
They cover the bord and fetch in the meate.

Sounes? burnt and skorcht who drest this meate?
Will. Forsouth John cooke.

[67]

*He throwes down the table and meate
and all, and beates them.*

Feran. Go, you villaines bringe you me such meate,
Out of my sight I say and beare it hence,
Come *Kate* wele have other meate provided,
Is there a fire in my chamber sir?
   San. I forsooth.   *Exit Ferando and Kate.*
   Manent servingmen and eate up all the meate.
   Tom. Sounes? I thinke of my conscience my Masters
Mad since he was maried.
   Will. I laft what a boxe he gave *Sander*
For pulling of his bootes.

Enter Ferando againe.

   San. I hurt his foote for the nonce man.
   Feran. Did you so you damned villaine.

He beates them all out againe.

This humor must I holde me to a while,
To bridle and hold backe my headstrong wife,
With curbes of hunger: ease: and want of sleepe,
Nor sleepe nor meate shall she injoie to night,
Ile mew her up as men do mew their hawkes,
And make her gentlie come unto the lure,
Were she as stuborne or as full of strength
As were the *Thracian* horse *Alcides* tamde,
That King *Egeus* fed with flesh of men,
Yet would I pull her downe and make her come
As hungry hawkes do flie unto there lure.   *Exit.*

Enter Aurelius and Valeria.

   Aurel. Valeria attend: I have a lovely love,
As bright as is the heaven cristalline,
As faire as is the milke white way of Jove,
As chast as *Phoebe* in her sommer sportes,
As softe and tender as the asure downe,

[68]

That circles *Cithereas* silver doves.
Her do I meane to make my lovely bride,
And in her bed to breath the sweete content,
That I thou knowst long time have aimed at.
Now *Valeria* it rests in thee to helpe
To compasse this, that I might gaine my love,
Which easilie thou maist performe at will,
If that the marchant which thou toldst me of,
Will as he sayd go to *Alfonsos* house,
And say he is my father, and there with all
Pas over certaine deedes of land to me,
That I thereby may gaine my hearts desire.
And he is promised reward of me.

    Val. Feare not my Lord Ile fetch him straight to you,
For hele do any thing that you command,
But tell me my Lord, is *Ferando* married then?

    Aurel. He is: and *Polidor* shortly shall be wed,
And he meanes to tame his wife erelong.

    Vale. He saies so.

    Aurel. Faith he's gon unto the taming schoole.

    Val. The taming schoole: why is there such a place?

    Aurel. I: and *Ferando* is the Maister of the schoole.

    Val. Thats rare: but what *decorum* dos he use?

    Aurel. Faith I know not: but by som odde devise
Or other, but come *Valeria* I long to see the man,
By whome we must comprise our plotted drift,
That I may tell him what we have to doo.

    Val. Then come my Lord and I will bring you to him
straight.

    Aurel. Agreed, then lets go.   *Exeunt*

    Enter *Sander and his Mistres.*

    San. Come Mistris.

    Kate. Sander I prethe helpe me to some meate,
I am so fainte that I can scarsely stande.

    San. I marry mistris but you know my maister

Has given me a charge that you must eate nothing,
But that which he himselfe giveth you.

    Kate. Why man thy Maister needs never know it.

    San. You say true indede: why looke you Mistris,
What say you to a peese of beeffe and mustard now?

    Kate. Why I say tis excellent meate, canst thou
helpe me to some?

    San. I, I could helpe you to some but that
I doubt the mustard is too collerick for you,
But what say you to a sheepes head and garlick?

    Kate. Why any thing, I care not what it be.

    San. I but the garlike I doubt will make your breath
stincke, and then my Maister will course me for letting
You eate it: But what say you to a fat Capon?

    Kate. Thats meate for a King sweet *Sander* helpe
Me to some of it.

    San. Nay berlady then tis too deere for us, we must
Not meddle with the Kings meate.

    Kate. Out villaine dost thou mocke me,
Take that for thy sawsinesse.

She beates him.

    San. Sounes are you so light fingerd with a murrin,
Ile keepe you fasting for it this two daies.

    Kate. I tell thee villaine Ile tear the flesh of
Thy face and eate it and thou prates to me thus.

    San. Here comes my Maister now hele course you.

Enter Ferando with a peece of meate uppon his
daggers point and Polidor with him.

    Feran. Se here *Kate* I have provided meate for thee,
Here take it: what ist not worthie thankes,
Goe sirra? take it awaie againe you shallbe
Thankefull for the next you have.

    Kate. Why I thanke you for it.

    Feran. Nay now tis not worth a pin go sirray and take
It hence I say.

[70]

San. Yes sir Ile Carrie it hence: Maister let her
Have none for she can fight as hungrie as she is.
   Pol. I pray you sir let it stand, for Ile eate
Some with her my selfe.
   Feran. Well sirra set it downe again.
   Kate. Nay nay I pray you let him take it hence,
And keepe it for your owne diete for Ile none,
Ile nere be beholding to you for your Meate,
I tell thee flatlie here unto the thy teethe
Thou shalt not keepe me nor feede me as thou list,
For I will home againe unto my fathers house.
   Feran. I, when you'r meeke and gentell but not
Before, I know your stomack is not yet come downe,
Therefore no marvell thou canste not eate,
And I will goe unto your Fathers house,
Come *Polidor* let us goe in againe,
And *Kate* come in with us I know ere longe,
That thou and I shall lovingly agree.   *Ex. Omnes*

          Enter *Aurelius Valeria and Phylotus*
                 the Marchant.

   Aurel. Now Senior *Phylotus*, we will go
Unto *Alfonsos* house, and be sure you say
As I did tell you, concerning the man
That dwells in *Cestus*, whose son I said I was,
For you doo very much resemble him,
And feare not: you may be bold to speake your mind.
   Phylo. I warrant you sir take you no care,
Ile use my selfe so cunning in the cause,
As you shall soone injoie your harts delight.
   Aurel. Thankes sweet *Phylotus*, then stay you here,
And I will go and fetch him hither straight.
Ho, Senior *Alfonso*: a word with you.

               Enter *Alfonso*.

   Alfon. Whose there? what *Aurelius* whats the matter
That you stand so like a stranger at the doore?

                    [71]

Aurel. My father sir is newly come to towne,
And I have brought him here to speake with you,
Concerning those matters that I tolde you of,
And he can certefie you of the truth.
    Alfon. Is this your father? you are welcome sir.
    Phylo. Thankes *Alfonso*, for thats your name I gesse,
I understand my son hath set his mind
And bent his liking to your daughters love,
And for because he is my only son,
And I would gladly that he should doo well,
I tell you sir, I not mislike his choise,
If you agree to give him your consent,
He shall have living to maintaine his state,
Three hundred poundes a yeere I will assure
To him and to his heyres, and if they do joyne,
And knit themselves in holy wedlockbande,
A thousand massie in gots of pure gold,
And twise as many bares of silver plate,
I freely give him; and in writing straight,
I will confirme what I have said in wordes.
    Alfon. Trust me I must commend your liberall mind,
And loving care you beare unto your son,
And here I give him freely my consent,
As for my daughter I thinke he knowes her mind,
And I will inlarge her dowrie for your sake.
And solemnise with joie your nuptiall rites,
But is this gentleman of *Cestus* too?
    Aurel. He is the *Duke* of *Cestus* thrise renowned son,
Who for the love his honour beares to me:
Hath thus accompanied me to this place.
    Alfonso. You weare to blame you told me not before,
Pardon me my Lord, for if I had knowne
Your honour had bin here in place with me,
I would have donne my dutie to your honour.
    Val. Thankes good *Alfonso*: but I did come to see
When as these marriage rites should be performed,
And if in these nuptialls you vouchsafe,

The taming of a Shrew

To honour thus the prince of *Cestus* frend,
In celebration of his spousall rites,
He shall remaine a lasting friend to you,
What saies *Aurelius* father.

    Phylo. I humbly thanke your honour good my Lord,
And ere we parte before your honor here
Shall articles of such content be drawne,
As twixt our houses and posterities,
Eternallie this league of peace shall last,
Inviolat and pure on either part.

    Alfonso. With all my heart, and if your honour please,
To walke along with us unto my house,
We will confirme these leagues of lasting love.

    Val. Come then Aurelius I will go with you. *Ex. omnes.*

        Enter *Ferando and Kate and Sander.*

    San. Master the haberdasher has brought my
Mistresse home her cappe here.

    Feran. Come hither sirra: what have you there?

    Habar. A velvet cappe sir and it please you.

    Feran. Who spoake for it? didst thou *Kate*?

    Kate. What if I did, come hither sirra, give me
The cap, Ile see if it will fit me.

        She sets it one hir head.

    Feran. O monstrous: why it becomes thee not,
Let me see it *Kate*: here sirra take it hence,
This cappe is out of fashion quite.

    Kate. The fashion is good inough: belike you,
Meane to make a foole of me.

    Feran. Why true he meanes to make a foole of thee,
To have thee put on such a curtald cappe,
sirra begon with it.

        Enter the *Taylor* with a gowne.

    San. Here is the *Taylor* too with my Mistris gowne.

[73]

Feran. Let me see it *Taylor*: what with cuts and jagges?
Sounes you villaine, thou hast spoiled the gowne.

Taylor. Why sir I made it as your man gave me direction,
You may reade the note here.

Feran. Come hither sirra: *Taylor* reade the note.

Taylor. Item a faire round compass cape.

San. I thats true.

Taylor. And a large truncke sleeve.

San. Thats a lie maister, I sayd two truncke sleeves.

Feran. Well sir goe forward.

Taylor. Item a loose bodied gowne.

San. Maister if ever I sayd loose bodies gowne,
Sew me in a seame and beate me to death,
With a bottome of browne thred.

Taylor. I made it as the note bad me.

San. I say the note lies in his throate and thou too,
And thou sayst it.

Taylor. Nay nay nere be so hot sirra, for I feare you not.

San. Doost thou heare *Taylor*, thou hast braved
Many men: brave not me.
Thou'st faste many men.

Taylor. Well sir.

San. Face not me Ile nether be faste nor braved
At thy handes I can tell thee.

Kate. Come come I like the fashion of it well enough,
Heres more a do then needs Ile have it I,
And if you do not like it hide your eies,
I thinke I shall have nothing by your will.

Feran. Go I say and take it up for your maisters use.

San. Souns: villaine not for thy life touch it not,
Souns, take up my mistris gowne to his
Maisters use?

Feran. Well sir: whats your conceit of it.

San. I have a deeper conceite in it then you
thinke for, take up my Mistris gowne
To his maisters use?

Feran. Tailor come hether: for this time take it

Hence againe, and Ile content thee for thy paines.
   Taylor. I thanke you sir.   *Exit Taylor.*
   Feran. Come *Kate* we now will go see thy fathers house
Even in these honest meane abilliments,
Our purses shallbe rich, our garments plaine.
To shrowd our bodies from the winter rage
And thats inough, what should we care for more
Thy sisters *Kate* to morrow must be wed,
And I have promised them thou shouldst be there
The morning is well up lets hast away,
It will be nine a clocke ere we come there.
   Kate. Nine a clock, why tis allreadie past two
In the after noone by all the clocks in the towne.
   Feran. I say tis but nine a clock in the morning.
   Kate. I say tis tow a clock in the after noone.
   Feran. It shall be nine then ere we go to your fathers,
Come backe againe, we will not go to day.
Nothing but crossing of me still,
Ile have you say as I doo ere you go.   *Exeunt omnes.*

      Enter *Polidor, Emelia, Aurelius and Philema.*

   Pol. Faire *Emelia* sommers sun bright Queene,
Brighter of hew then is the burning clime,
Where *Phoebus* in his bright æquator sits,
Creating gold and pressious minneralls,
What would *Emelia* doo? if I were forst
To leave faire *Athens* and to range the world.
   Eme. Should thou assay to scale the seate of Jove,
Mounting the suttle ayrie regions
Or be snacht up as erste was *Ganimed,*
Love should give winges unto my swift desires,
And prune my thoughts that I would follow thee,
Or fall and perish as did *Icarus.*
   Aurel. Sweetly resolved faire *Emelia,*
But would *Phylema* say as much to me,
If I should aske a question now of thee,
What if the duke of *Cestus* only son,

[75]

Which came with me unto your fathers house,
Should seeke to git *Phylemas* love from me,
And make thee Duches of that stately towne,
Wouldst thou not then forsake me for his love?

   Phyle. Not for great *Neptune*, no nor *Jove* himselfe,
Will *Phylema* leave *Aurelius* love,
Could he install me *Empres* of the world,
Or make me Queene and guidres of the heavens,
Yet would I not exchange thy love for his,
Thy company is poore *Philemas* heaven,
And without thee, heaven were hell to me.

   Eme. And should my love as erste did *Hercules*
Attempt to passe the burning valtes of hell,
I would with piteous lookes and pleasing wordes,
As once did *Orpheus* with his harmony,
And ravishing sound of his melodious harpe,
Intreate grim *Pluto* and of him obtaine,
That thou mightest go and safe retourne againe.

   Phyle. And should my love as earst *Leander* did,
Attempte to swimme the boyling helispont
For *Heros* love: no towers of brasse should hold
But I would follow thee through those raging flouds,
With lockes dishevered and my brest all bare,
With bended knees upon *Abidas* shoore,
I would with smokie sighes and brinish teares,
Importune *Neptune* and the watry Gods,
To send a guard of silver sealed *Dolphyns*,
With sounding *Tritons* to be our convoy,
And to transport us safe unto the shore,
Whilst I would hang about thy lovely necke,
Redoubling kisse on kisse upon thy cheekes,
And with our pastime still the swelling waves.

   Eme. Should *Polidor* as great *Achilles* did,
Onely imploy himselfe to follow armes,
Like to the warlike *Amazonian* Queene,
Pentheselea Hectors paramore,
Who soyld the bloudie *Pirrhus* murderous greeke,

[76]

Ile thrust my selfe amongst the thickest throngs,
And with my utmost force assist my love.

Phyle. Let *Eole* storme: be mild and quiet thou,
Let *Neptune* swell, be *Aurelius* calme and pleased,
I care not I, betide what may betide,
Let fates and fortune doo the worst they can,
I recke them not: they not discord with me,
Whilst that my love and I do well agree.

Aurel. Sweet *Phylema* bewties mynerall,
From whence the sun exhales his glorious shine,
And clad the heaven in thy reflected raies,
And now my liefest love, the time drawes nie,
That *Himen* mounted in his saffron robe,
Must with his torches waight upon thy traine,
As *Hellens* brothers on the horned Moone,
Now *Juno* to thy number shall I adde,
The fairest bride that ever Marchant had.

Pol. Come faire *Emelia* the preeste is gon,
And at the church your father and the reste,
Do stay to see our marriage rites performde,
And knit in sight of heaven this *Gordian* knot.
That teeth of fretting time may nere untwist,
Then come faire love and gratulate with me,
This daies content and sweet solemnity.   *Ex. Omnes*

Slie Sim must they be married now?
Lord. I my Lord.

Enter *Ferando and Kate and Sander.*

Slie. Looke *Sim* the foole is come againe now.
Feran. Sirra go fetch our horsses forth, and bring
Them to the backe gate presentlie.
San. I will sir I warrant you,   *Exit Sander.*
Feran. Come *Kate* the Moone shines cleere to night
methinkes.
Kate. The moone? why husband you are deceivd
It is the sun.

[77]

Feran. Yet againe: come backe againe it shall be
The moone ere we come at your fathers.
   Kate. Why Ile say as you say it is the moone.
   Feran. Jesus save the glorious moone.
   Kate. Jesus save the glorious moone.
   Feran. I am glad *Kate* your stomack is come downe,
I know it well thou knowest it is the sun,
But I did trie to see if thou wouldst speake,
And crosse me now as thou hast donne before,
And trust me *kate* hadst thou not named the moone,
We had gon back againe as sure as death,
But soft whose this thats comming here.

Enter the Duke of Cestus alone.

   Duke. Thus all alone from *Cestus* am I come,
And left my princelie courte and noble traine,
To come to *Athens*, and in this disguise,
To see what course my son *Aurelius* takes,
But stay, heres some it may be Travells thether,
Good sir can you derect me the way to *Athens*?

Ferando speakes to the olde man.

Faire lovely maide yoong and affable,
More cleere of hew and far more beautifull,
Then pretious *Sardonix* or purple rockes,
Of *Amithests* or glistering *Hiasinthe*,
More amiable farre then is the plain,
Where glistring *Cepherus* in silver boures,
Gaseth upon the Giant *Andromede*,
Sweet *Kate* entertaine this lovely woman.
   Duke. I thinke the man is mad he calles me a woman.
   Kate. Faire lovely lady, bright and Christalline,
Bewteous and stately as the eie-traind bird,
As glorious as the morning washt with dew,
Within whose eies she takes her dawningbeames,
And golden sommer sleepes upon thy cheekes,

[78]

Wrap up thy radiations in some cloud,
Least that thy bewty make this stately towne,
Inhabitable like the burning *Zone*,
With sweet reflections of thy lovely face.
    Duke. What is she mad to? or is my shape transformd,
That both of them perswade me I am a woman,
But they are mad sure, and therefore Ile begon,
And leave their companies for fear of harme,
And unto *Athens* hast to seeke my son.

                          Exit Duke.

    Feran. Why so *Kate* this was friendly done of thee,
And kindly too: why thus must we two live,
One minde, one heart, and one content for both,
This good old man dos thinke that we are mad,
And glad he is I am sure, that he is gonne,
But come sweet *Kate* for we will after him,
And now perswade him to his shape againe.

                          Ex. omnes.

      Enter *Alfonso and Phylotus and Valeria,*
      Polidor, Emelia, Aurelius and Phylema.

    Alfon. Come lovely sonnes your marriage rites perfoimed,
Lets hie us home to see what cheere we have,
I wonder that *Ferando* and his wife
Comes not to see this great solemnitie.
    Pol. No marvell if *Ferando* be away,
His wife I think hath troubled so his wits,
That he remaines at home to keepe them warme,
For forward wedlocke as the proverbe sayes,
Hath brought him to his nightcappe long agoe.
    Phylo. But *Polidor* let my son and you take heede,
That *Ferando* say not ere long as much to you,
And now *Alfonso* more to shew my love,
If unto *Cestus* you do send your ships,
My selfe will fraught them with *Arabian* silkes,

[79]

Rich affrick spices *Arras* counter poines,
Muske *Cassia*: sweet smelling *Ambergreece*,
Pearle, curroll, christall, jett, and ivorie,
To gratulate the favors of my son,
And friendlie love that you have shone to him.
Vale. And for to honour him and this faire bride,

Enter the *Duke of Cestus.*

Ile yerly send you from my fathers courte,
Chests of refind suger severally,
Ten tunns of tunis wine, sucket sweet druges,
To celibrate and solemnise this day,
And custome free your marchants shall converse:
And interchange the profits of your land,
Sending you gold for brasse, silver for leade,
Casses of silke for packes of woll and cloth,
To binde this friendship and confirme this league.
  Duke. I am glad sir that you would be so franke,
Are you become the *Duke* of *Cestus* son,
And revels with my treasure in the towne,
Base villaine that thus dishonorest me.
  Val. Sounes it is the *Duke* what shall I doo,
Dishonour thee why, knowst thou what thou saist?
  Duke. Her's no villaine: he will not know me now,
But what say you? have you forgot me too?
  Phylo. Why sir, are you acquainted with my son?
  Duke. With thy son? no trust me if he be thine,
I pray you sir who am I?
  Aurel. Pardon me father: humblie on my knees,
I do intreat your grace to heare me speake.
  Duke. Peace villaine: lay handes on them,
And send them to prison straight.

Phylotus and Valeria runnes away.
Then *Slie* speakes.

Slie. I say wele have no sending to prison.

[80]

The taming of a Shrew

Lord. My Lord this is but the play, theyre but in jest.

Slie. I tell thee *Sim* wele have no sending,
To prison thats flat: why *Sim* am not I *Don Christo Vary?*
Therefore I say they shall not go to prison.

Lord. No more they shall not my Lord,
They be run away.

Slie. Are they run away *Sim?* thats well,
Then gis some more drinke, and let them play againe.

Lord. Here my Lord.

Slie drinkes and then falls a sleepe.

Duke. Ah trecherous boy that durst presume,
To wed thy selfe without thy fathers leave,
I sweare by fayre *Cintheas* burning rayes,
By *Merops* head and by seaven mouthed *Nile*,
Had I but knowne ere thou hadst wedded her,
Were in thy brest the worlds immortall soule,
This angrie sword should rip thy hatefull chest,
And hewd thee smaller then the *Libian* sandes,
Turne hence thy face: oh cruell impious boy,
Alfonso I did not thinke you would presume,
To mach your daughter with my princely house,
And nere make me acquainted with the cause.

Alfon. My Lord by heavens I sweare unto your grace,
I knew none other but *Valeria* your man,
Had bin the *Duke* of *Cestus* noble son,
Nor did my daughter I dare sweare for her.

Duke. That damned villaine that hath deluded me,
Whome I did send guide unto my son,
Oh that my furious force could cleave the earth,
That I might muster bands of hellish feendes,
To rack his heart and teare his impious soule.
The ceaselesse turning of celestiall orbes,
Kindles not greater flames in flitting aire,
Then passionate anguish of my raging brest,

Aurel. Then let my death sweet father end your griefe,

[81]

For I it is that thus have wrought your woes,
Then be revengd on me for here I sweare,
That they are innocent of what I did,
Oh had I charge to cut of *Hydraes* hed,
To make the toplesse *Alpes* a champion field,
To kill untamed monsters with my sword,
To travell dayly in the hottest sun,
And watch in winter when the nightes be colde,
I would with gladnesse undertake them all,
And thinke the paine but pleasure that I felt,
So that my noble father at my returne,
Would but forget and pardon my offence,
 Phile. Let me intreat your grace upon my knees,
To pardon him and let my death discharge
The heavy wrath your grace hath vowd gainst him.
 Pol. And good my Lord let us intreat your grace,
To purge your stomack of this Melancholy,
Taynt not your princely mind with grief my Lord,
But pardon and forgive these lovers faults,
That kneeling crave your gratious favor here.
 Emel. Great prince of *Cestus*, let a womans wordes,
Intreat a pardon in your lordly brest,
Both for your princely son, and us my Lord.
 Duke. Aurelius stand up I pardon thee,
I see that vertue will have enemies,
And fortune willbe thwarting honour still,
And you faire virgin too I am content,
To accept you for my daughter since tis don,
And see you princely usde in *Cestus* courte.
 Phyle. Thankes good my Lord and I no longer live,
Then I obey and honour you in all:
 Alfon. Let me give thankes unto your royall grace,
For this great honor don to me and mine,
And if your grace will walke unto my house,
I will in humblest maner I can, show
The eternall service I doo owe your grace.
 Duke. Thanks good *Alfonso*: but I came alone,

[82]

The taming of a Shrew

And not as did beseeme the *Cestian Duke,*
Nor would I have it knowne within the towne,
That I was here and thus without my traine,
But as I came alone so will I go,
And leave my son to solemnise his feast,
And ere't belong Ile come againe to you,
And do him honour as beseemes the son
Of mightie *Jerobell* the *Cestian Duke,*
Till when Ile leave you, Farwell *Aurelius.*
    Aurel. Not yet my Lord, Ile bring you to your ship.

               Exeunt Omnes.

               Slie sleepes.

    Lord. Whose within there? come hither sirs my Lords
A sleepe againe: go take him easily up,
And put him in his one apparell againe,
And lay him in the place where we did find him,
Just underneath the alehouse side below,
But see you wake him not in any case.
    Boy. It shall be don my Lord come helpe to beare him
hence,   *Exit.*

    Enter Ferando, Aurelius and Polidor
    and his boy and Valeria and Sander.

    Feran. Come gentlemen now that suppers donne,
How shall we spend the time till we go to bed?
    Aurel. Faith if you will in triall of our wives,
Who will come sownest at their husbands call.
    Pol. Nay then *Ferando* he must needes sit out,
For he may call I thinke till he be weary,
Before his wife will come before she list.
    Feran. Tis well for you that have such gentle wives,
Yet in this triall will I not sit out,
It may be *Kate* will come as soone as yours.
    Aurel. My wife comes soonest for a hundred pound.
    Pol. I take it: Ile lay as much to youres,

That my wife comes as soone as I do send.
   Aurel. How now *Ferando* you dare not lay belike.
   Feran. Why true I dare not lay indeede;
But how, so little mony on so sure a thing,
A hundred pound: why I have layd as much
Upon my dogge, in running at a Deere,
She shall not come so farre for such a trifle,
But will you lay five hundred markes with me,
And whose wife soonest comes when he doth call,
And shewes her selfe most loving unto him,
Let him injoye the wager I have laid,
Now what say you? dare you adventure thus?
   Pol. I weare it a thousand pounds I durst presume
On my wives love: and I will lay with thee.

Enter Alfonso.

   Alfon. How now sons what in conference so hard,
May I without offence, know where abouts.
   Aurel. Faith father a waighty cause about our wives
Five hundred markes already we have layd,
And he whose wife doth shew most love to him,
He must injoie the wager to himselfe.
   Alfon. Why then *Ferando* he is sure to lose,
I promise thee son thy wife will hardly come,
And therefore I would not wish thee lay so much.
   Feran. Tush father were it ten times more,
I durst adventure on my lovely *Kate*,
But if I lose Ile pay, and so shall you.
   Aurel. Upon mine honour if I loose Ile pay.
   Pol. And so will I upon my faith I vow.
   Feran. Then sit we downe and let us send for them.
   Alfon. I promise thee *Ferando* I am afraid thou wilt lose
   Aurel. Ile send for my wife first, *Valeria*
Go bid your Mistris come to me.
   Val. I will my Lord.

Exit Valeria.

[84]

Aurel. Now for my hundred pound.
Would any lay ten hundred more with me,
I know I should obtaine it by her love.
   Feran. I pray God you have not laid too much already.
   Aurel. Trust me *Ferando* I am sure you have,
For you I dare presume have lost it all.

Enter *Valeria* againe.

Now sirra what saies your mistris?
   Val. She is something busie but shele come anon.
   Feran. Why so, did not I tell you this before,
She is busie and cannot come.
   Aurel. I pray God your wife send you so good an answere
She may be busie yet she sayes shele come.
   Feran. Well well: *Polidor* send you for your wife.
   Pol. Agreed *Boy* desire your mistris to come hither.
   Boy. I will sir   *Ex. Boy.*
   Feran. I so so he desiers her to come.
   Alfon. *Polidor* I dare presume for thee,
I thinke thy wife will not deny to come.
And I do marvell much *Aurelius*,
That your wife came not when you sent for her.

Enter the *Boy* againe.

   Pol. Now wheres your Mistris?
   Boy. She bad me tell you that she will not come,
And you have any businesse, you must come to her.
   Feran. Oh monstrous intollerable presumption,
Worse than a blasing starre, or snow at midsommer,
Earthquakes or any thing unseasonable,
She will not come: but he must come to her.
   Pol. Well sir I pray you lets here what
Answere your wife will make.
   Feran. Sirra, command your Mistris to come
To me presentlie.   *Exit Sander.*
   Aurel. I thinke my wife for all she did not come,

[85]

Will prove most kinde for now I have no feare,
For I am sure *Ferandos* wife, she will not come.
  Feran. The mores the pittie: then I must lose.

Enter *Kate* and *Sander.*

But I have won for see where *Kate* doth come.
  Kate. Sweet husband did you send for me?
  Feran. I did my love I sent for thee to come,
Come hither *Kate*, whats that upon thy head
  Kate. Nothing husband but my cap I thinke.
  Feran. Pull it of and treade it under thy feete,
Tis foolish I will have thee weare it.

She takes of her cap and treads on it.

  Pol. Oh wonderfull metamorphosis.
  Aurel. This is a wonder: almost past beleefe.
  Feran. This is a token of her true love to me,
And yet Ile trie her further you shall see,
Come hither *Kate* where are thy sisters.
  Kate. They be sitting in the bridall chamber.
  Feran. Fetch them hither and if they will not come,
Bring them perforce and make them come with thee.
  Kate. I will.
  Alfon. I promise thee *Ferando* I would have sworne,
Thy wife would nere have donne so much for thee.
  Feran. But you shall see she will do more then this,
For see where she brings her sisters forth by force.

Enter *Kate* thrusting *Phylema* and *Emelia* before her,
and makes them come unto their husbands call.

Kate See husband I have brought them both.
  Feran. Tis well don *Kate.*
  Eme. I sure and like a loving peece, your worthy
To have great praise for this attempt.
  Phyle. I for making a foole of her selfe and us.
  Aurel. Beshrew thee *Phylema*, thou hast

[86]

Lost me a hundred pound to night.
For I did lay that thou wouldst first have come.
    Pol. But thou *Emelia* hast lost me a great deale more.
    Eme. You might have kept it better then,
Who bad you lay?
    Feran. Now lovely *Kate* before there husbands here,
I prethe tell unto these hedstrong women,
What dutie wives doo owe unto their husbands.
    Kate. Then you that live thus by your pompered wills,
Now list to me and marke what I shall say,
Theternall power that with his only breath,
Shall cause this end and this beginning frame,
Not in time, nor before time, but with time, confusd,
For all the course of yeares, of ages, moneths,
Of seasons temperate, of dayes and houres,
Are tund and stopt, by measure of his hand,
The first world was, a forme, without a forme,
A heape confusd a mixture all deformd,
A gulfe of gulfes, a body bodiles,
Where all the elements were orderles,
Before the great commander of the world,
The King of Kings the glorious God of heaven,
Who in six daies did frame his heavenly worke,
And made all things to stand in perfit course.
Then to his image he did make a man.
Olde *Adam* and from his side a sleepe,
A rib was taken, of which the Lord did make,
The woe of man so termd by *Adam* then,
Woman for that, by her came sinne to us,
And for her sin was *Adam* doomd to die,
As *Sara* to her husband, so should we,
Obey them, love them, keepe, and nourish them,
If they by any meanes doo want our helpes,
Laying our handes under theire feete to tread,
If that by that we, might procure there ease,
And for a president Ile first begin,
And lay my hand under my husbands feete

She laies her hand under her husbands feete

Feran. Inough sweet, the wager thou hast won,
And they I am sure cannot denie the same.
Alfon. I Ferando the wager thou hast won,
And for to shew thee how I am pleasd in this,
A hundred poundes I freely give thee more,
Another dowry for another daughter,
For she is not the same she was before.
Feran. Thankes sweet father, gentlemen godnight
For *Kate* and I will leave you forto night,
Tis *Kate* and I am wed, and you are sped.
Andso farwell for we will to our beds.

Exit Ferando and Kate and Sander.

Alfon. Now *Aurelius* what say you to this?
Aurel. Beleeve me father I rejoice to see,
Ferando and his wife so lovingly agree.

*Exit Aurelius and Phylema and
Alfonso and Valeria.*

Eme. How now *Polidor* in a dump, what sayst thou
man?
Pol. I say thou art a shrew.
Eme. Thats better then a sheepe.
Pol. Well since tis don let it go, come lets in.

Exit Polidor and Emelia.

Then enter two bearing of *Slie* in his
Owne apparrell againe, and leaves him
Where they found him, and then goes out.
Then enter the *Tapster.*

Tapster. Now that the darkesome night is overpast,
And dawning day apeares in cristall sky,
Now must I hast abroad: but soft whose this?
What *Slie* oh wondrous hath he laine here allnight,

[88]

Ile wake him, I thinke he's starved by this,
But that his belly was so stuft with ale,
What how *Slie*, Awake for shame.

    Slie. *Sim* gis some more wine: whats all the
Plaiers gon: am not I a Lord?

    Tapster. A Lord with a murrin: come art thou
dronken still?

    Slie. Whose this? *Tapster*, oh Lord sirra, I have had
The bravest dreame to night, that ever thou
Hardest in all thy life.

    Tapster. I marry but you had best get you home.
For your wife will course you for dreming here to night,

    Slie. Will she? I know now how to tame a shrew,
I dreamt upon it all this night till now,
And thou hast wakt me out of the best dreame
That ever I had in my life, but Ile to my
Wife presently and tame her too
And if she anger me.

    Tapster. Nay tarry *Slie* for Ile go home with thee,
And heare the rest that thou hast dreamt to night.

Exeunt Omnes.

FINIS

Endnotes

Title: 'Historie' could be used generally in Elizabethan language with an implication closer to modern 'story' than to 'history', though usually implying a story of a representative or exemplary kind. Bartholemew the Page in *The Taming of the Shrew* defines comedy as 'a kind of history'. 'Pleasant', and 'conceited' ('enjoyable' and 'clever, witty'), of course, suggest the conventions of comedy.

Page 43

The male Tapster in this text replaces the female Hostess in *The Taming of the Shrew*. The latter version foregrounds a conflict between female authority and masculine resistance. In *The Taming of a Shrew* the conflict is more class- than gender-based, and is resolved in the play's conclusion by the establishing of a masculine freemasonry between Tapster and Slie:

Tapster: For your wife will course you for dreming here to night,
Slie: Will she? I know now how to tame a shrew . . . (p. 89)

panch: paunch, stomach.

Tilly vally: a meaningless expletive.

by crisee: by Christ.

fese: fix, 'do for'.

Fils the tother pot: Slie's speech is characterised by such phonetic indications of common dialect ('Fill us [i.e. for me] the other pot').

Instegation: 'instigation', i.e. 'no one drives me to it but myself'.

The Lord quotes directly from Marlowe's *Dr Faustus* (see Introduction, above, p. 24.

Orion: giant in Greek mythology, murdered by Artemis and transported to the sky as a constellation.

Endnotes

antarticke: antarctic.

Welkin: sky.

Page 44

Cupple: couple.

boord: board.

devisde: carries associations of trickery and of dramatic improvisation.

Al fellows now: 'all mates together', i.e. the Lord must be indistinguishable from the servants; but also that they are all equally participants in the practical joke. The term 'fellow' denoted lower class status than 'man'. The Lord transforms himself by cross-dressing of class into a common man, as Slie is transformed into a Lord.

sutes: suits (of clothes).

Page 45

fit: adopt a character, assume a role.

San: it is clear from the speech heading that the speaker here is the actor who plays Sander (i.e. the travelling players' clown), who, with his malapropisms ('Tragicall' and 'comoditie', for 'tragedy' and 'comedy') and his chauvinistic humour (see below), immediately establishes a tone of broad comedy.

The inner play is here identified, much more explicitly than in *The Taming of the Shrew*, as an object lesson in male chauvinism.

scuse: excuse.

Page 46

to: too.

properties: part of the series of running gags referring to Marlowe's *Dr Faustus*, which must have required in performance such a property to represent 'Faustus' limbs, / All torn asunder by the hand of death' (XX, 6–7). Compare also IV, 8–10: 'I know the villain's out of service, and so hungry that I know he would give his soul to the devil for a shoulder of mutton, though it were blood-raw'.

(S.D.) *Enter two . . .* The parallel stage direction in *The Taming of the Shrew* reads:

[91]

Endnotes

Enter aloft the drunkard with attendants, some with apparel, Bason and Ewer, and other appurtenances, and Lord

For a comparative discussion, and for the staging problems presented by *The Taming of the Shrew*'s version, see Graham Holderness, *Shakespeare in Performance: the Taming of the Shrew* (Manchester: Manchester University Press, 1989), pp. 4–6.

earst: earlier.

small ale . . . wine: the two types of drink map the class division between the social environments of Slie and the Lord.

Pegasus: winged horse of Greek mythology. Compare *Tamburlaine*, One, 1.2.94: 'Mounted on steeds swifter than Pegasus'.

Page 47

Row: roe deer.

moorned: mourned.

gratulate: welcome, give thanks for (cp. modern 'congratulate').

frantike: frantic, crazy.

Page 48

flout: mock, jeer or quote sarcastically.

Athens: chosen perhaps for its academic associations, but useful also as an appropriate ground of classical reference. The mercantile context is associated both with Athens and with the city of Sestos ('Cestus'). The Padua of *The Taming of the Shrew* also provides the scene for both intellectual and commercial contexts.

Cestus: Sestos, which faced Abydos across the Hellespont.

Leander: Leander drowned in the Hellespont while swimming to reach his lover Hero. Compare Marlowe's long narrative poem *Hero and Leander* (1598).

renowmed: renowned.

Casar: Julius Caesar.

vouchsafe: grant, bestow.

what dames are these . . . : Aurelius echoes Marlowe's *Tamburlaine*, One, 3.3.118, 120: 'Fairer than rocks of pearl and precious stone . . . Whose eyes are brighter than the lamps of heaven.'

[92]

Endnotes

Page 49
compasse: encompass.

skould: scold, shrew.

sped . . . speed: 'until she's got rid of, no one else can succeed'.

Page 50
The image of honor: cp. *Tamburlaine,* One, 5.1.75, 78–9: 'Image of honour and nobility . . . In whose sweet person is compris'd the sum / Of nature's skill and heavenly majesty'.

fit: the idea of suitability, or of a parity of equal forces, is implicitly connected here with the notion of assuming a role (cp. above, p. 91, note on page 45).

match: a term associated with the arrangement of marriage, but here also suggesting a game or contest between equal contenders.

the center of my soule: she is the 'center' of his soul, as the earth was thought to be the centre of the universe. Compare *Tamburlaine,* Two, 2.4.84: 'darts do pierce the centre of my soul'.

Grecian Helena: Helen of Troy.

Tenedos: an island off the coast of Troy. Compare *Tamburlaine,* Two, 2.4.87–8: 'Helen, whose beauty summoned Greece to arms / And drew a thousand ships to Tenedos'.

traffike: trade, commerce.

publike schooles: i.e. the Athenian academy; usually referring to a university institution.

clothed thus in your attire: the frequent allusions to clothes and to cross-dressing link the conventions of comic plot to the metadramatic practice of the Elizabethan stage (see Introduction, pp. 22–3).

Page 51
blew coat: Saunders wears the blue livery coat of his master (see below, p. 54 and note).

marke: units of currency.

in the vaine: in the van, i.e. in the lead, first in the queue.

woe: woo.

going to this geere: 'geere' could signify any kind of equipment or apparatus, thus 'getting on with this job'. OED records a meaning 'organs of generation', which would also be apposite.

bonie: bonny.

venter: venture.

woo with skoulding: court her by quarrelling.

toot: to it.

Page 52

my ten commandments: she will impose authority by using the force of her fingers, i.e. punch him in the face.

In faith sir no the woodcock wants his taile: the woodcock was a bird proverbially easy to snare; but Kate's 'taile' is not available for catching.

Page 53

(S.D.) She turns aside and speakes: this 'aside', by means of which Kate both testifies to a complex subjectivity separable from her public persona and indicates her voluntary entry into a contest with Ferando, presents a striking contrast with *The Taming of the Shrew*.

match him: carrying associations of arranged marriage, but signifying primarily an entry into competition, a 'match' which Kate hopes to win or draw.

or else his manhoods good: 'if I don't equal him, he must be much of a man'. Compare p. 66, where Aurelius uses the same phrase *of Kate*, attributing manly virtue to a woman: 'Her manhood then is good I do beleeve'. The suggestion is in its context ironic, but taken together with Kate's aside seems to allow for the possibility of a 'manhood' shared between the sexes.

woode: wooed.

chud: (dialect) 'I would'.

Page 54

head men of the parish: 'head man' has from very early times been used to identify various types of community leadership.

liverie cote: Sander's 'blew cote' represents his master's livery, the household insignia of a servant.

slash it out and swash it out: terms from fencing, used here to indicate

[94]

Endnotes

fashionable bravado; cp. 'swashbuckle', literally to give violent blows on a shield, figuratively to swagger.

Ile scarce put up: 'I will hardly condescend to answer to anything as plain as my own name'.

takes it upon me: stand upon my dignity.

pantoflles: high-heeled cork-soled chopins, often alluded to in phrases meaning 'to stand on one's dignity'.

out of all crie: a favourite slang phrase of Saunder's, meaning here something like 'as big as you please'.

a late: of late, recently.

kno you who we are: Saunder uses a kind of 'royal plural' to enhance his imaginary status.

Page 55

Ecce signum: religious expression, 'behold the sign' (pointing to his livery coat).

Alpine Christall mould: the snow-covered earth of the Alps.

Page 56

buttrie: kitchen, larder.

Musition: musician.

fit his turne: suit his purpose, with the usual cross-reference to 'fit' as the assumption of a dramatic role.

steele: steal, sneak.

worke . . . play: literally 'make them work while she plays her music', but also 'do what she pleases while they do her bidding'. Kate is both forceful (towards her sisters, who 'work') and wilful (in respect of herself, who can 'play').

agreese: agree together, 'are getting on'.

skarse: scarcely.

skoller: scholar, pupil.

Page 57

gentlewomen: presumably Valeria in his music-master disguise looks to

Endnotes

Slie like a woman. In the 1590s both actors were of course boys. See Introduction, p. 15.

Page 58

that thing that's your delight: Valeria initiates with this pleasantry ('whatever pleases you most') a string of sexual quibbles.

If that sweet mistresse: 'if it's your pleasure to have me hide my face in some "case", let it be your cunt; you would then have control over my cock ("command a greater thing") even though the position would be ten times more humiliating for me than putting my face into a lute-case.'

coxcombe: fool's cap.

Page 59

clap your fiddle on your face: 'I'll slap my cunt (that which you want to "fiddle" with) on your face' (compare 'do you bid me kisse your arse?').

At the vengeance: gone to the devil.

berlady: by Our Lady.

Prometheus: Titan of Greek myth who resisted the Olympians and acquired for humanity the fire that was withheld from them in vengeance by Zeus.

Page 60

Phebus: Phoebus Apollo, Greek god of the sun.

Helispont: stretch of water between the cities of Sestos and Abydos. See above, p. 92, note on p. 48.

filde: filled.

Juno: consort of Jupiter and goddess of marriage.

Page 61

carde: care.

baselie attired: through the adjective 'baselie' the emphasis falls on the low social status and apparent poverty of Ferando's appearance. Petruchio's costume in *The Taming of the Shrew* is much more carnivalesque and 'fantastic'.

were: wear.

Page 62

tirde: attired, dressed.

[96]

Endnotes

Diana: Diana, Roman goddess of the moon and of hunting.

Apenis: the Apennine mountains.

groes: grows.

Boreas: in Greek myth the North Wind.

Ibis: sacred bird of the Egyptians.

Zanthus: a river.

Simies . . . Idas feete: Mount Ida on the island of Crete.

Median: fashioned by the Medes.

Russian stemes: ships made of Russian timber.

Plous up huge forrowes: plough up huge furrows.

Terren Maine: the Mediterranean.

Page 63

you have many boies with such / Pickadevantes: 'how many boys do you see with fashionable beards like mine?' 'Boy' indicated both youth and low social status.

venson: venison.

marchpaines: marzipans.

thums me: handles me roughly.

Page 64

my / Timber: 'my stick will communicate my meaning exactly right across your forehead'.

Imperfecksious . . . supernodicall: pseudo-learned language.

invade: cut into.

Ile barre: I draw the line at.

Coller: choler, anger.

Page 65

curtall: horse with a docked tail, small nag.

lavender: malapropism for 'provender'.

stand not on termes: 'don't insist on a strict legal interpretation'.

Endnotes

Page 66

Her manhood: see p. 53 above, and note p. 94.

Her toung will walke: 'even if she keeps her hands off him, her tongue will never be still'.

grone: grown.

holde her in: the implicit metaphor from riding is one of a series of allusions to 'taming' a woman as parallel to the forceful controlling of a horse (cp. Introduction, above p. 26).

And of what worth your friendship: 'I won't go into the various opinions about how much I value your friendship; but as I haven't yet repaid the kindnesses you've already done me, they will be settled in full when the appropriate opportunity arises'. Aurelius seems to be affecting a tone of magniloquent nonsense.

Page 67

adsum: I am here.

skorcht: scorched.

Page 68

Manent servingmen: the servingmen remain.

bridle . . . hold backe . . . curbes: the metaphors all refer to the reining in of a horse with bridle and bit ('curb'); but there is also an implicit reference to the 'scold's bridle' (see Introduction, p. 26).

ease: the placing of this word, and the punctuation, are difficult to interpret, as though 'ease' is misplaced in the line ('want of ease and sleep' would make perfect sense). On the other hand, Ferando may be proposing to punish Kate with 'ease' ('respite') from sexual intercourse: see *Introduction*, p. 25. This is one of very few points in this text where the original fails to make immediate good sense to a modern reading.

mew: to confine a hawk while the bird is moulting.

Thracian . . . Alcides . . . King Egeus: the text repeats Marlowe's error (*Tamburlaine*, Two, 4.312–18): Diomedes of Thrace owned the man-eating mares subdued by Hercules (Alcides) as his eighth labour.

Phoebe: Diana, Roman goddess of hunting.

asure: azure.

[98]

Endnotes

Citherea: Aphrodite, so called from the Phoenician trading-post Cythera, which formed one of the originating sites for the cult of the goddess of love.

decorum: discipline, system of training.

comprise our plotted drift: put together our intended plan.

collerick: likely to incite anger.

Capon: chicken.

berlady: by Our Lady.

sawsinesse: sauciness, insolence.

murrin: plague, disease.

course: curse.

Ex. Omnes: all go out.

Senior: signor.

curtald: 'cur-tailed', dog-eared.

jagges: ornamental cutting, or slashing of material to reveal a coloured lining.

round compast: full-cut.

truncke sleeve: full sleeve.

loose bodied gowne: a dress full in the bodice. Sander supplies his own meaning in 'a loose bodies gowne', a dress for a loose woman.

bottome: spool, bobbin.

braved . . . brave: the tailor has adorned many men with finery; Sander puns on the other meaning of 'brave', 'defy'.

faste . . . Face: trimmed . . . threaten.

take up my Mistris gowne: Ferando suggests that the tailor pick up the dress and take it away for his master to make some other use of. Sanders assumes that he means 'lift up Katherina's dress so his master may use her sexually'.

Page 75

abilliments: habiliments, clothes.

tow: two.

Jove: Jupiter, king of the Olympian gods.

Ganimed: Ganymede, a beautiful youth snatched by an eagle and brought to Olympus to become the favourite of Zeus and cupbearer to the gods.

prune: trim or dress a bird's feather's, 'plume'.

Icarus: son of the inventor Daedalus, killed when his manufactured wings melted from the heat of the sun.

Page 76

Neptune: sea-god in Roman mythology.

Hercules . . . the burning valtes of hell: one of the 'twelve labours of Hercules' was that of descending into hell and returning with the three-headed dog Cerberus.

Orpheus: Orpheus, legendary hero and miraculous musician, also descended into Hell to rescue from death his beloved Eurydice. He was able to charm Hades (*Pluto*), god of the underworld, into releasing her by the power of his playing.

Leander . . . Heros . . . helispont: see above p. 48, and note on p. 92.

dishevered: dishevelled.

Abidas: Abydos, across the Hellespont from Sestos.

Tritons: mythical sea-monsters, half-man and half-fish.

Achilles: Greek hero who fought at Troy, killing Hector and being killed by Paris.

Amazonian Queene, / Pentheselea Hectors paramore: Pentheselea was queen of the Amazons, a race of warrior women, who assisted the Trojans at the siege of Troy. She was loved by Hector and killed by Achilles.

Pirrhus: Pyrrhus, Greek warrior who fought at Troy, bested by Pentheselea.

Endnotes

Page 77
Eole: Aeolus, mythological guardian of the winds.

Himen: Hymen, Roman god of marriage.

Hellens brothers: Castor and Pollux; in myth twin brothers to Helen of Troy and Clytemnestra; in astronomy a constellation of twin stars.

Gordian knot: an apparently inextricable legendary knot, cut through by Alexander the Great.

Page 78
Sardinox: precious stone, a variety of onyx.

Hiasinthe: precious stone, possibly the sapphire.

Cepherus: Cephisus, river reputed to have its source on Mount Parnassus.

Andromede: Andromeda, daughter of Cepheus and Cassiopeia, rescued from human sacrifice by Perseus.

Page 79
burning Zone: equator.

Page 80
Arras counter poines: counterpanes from Arras, in northern France.

Muske Cassia: perfume from the fragrant Cassia bush.

Ambergreece: wax-like substance, found in whales and used in perfumery.

shone: shown.

yerly: annually.

sucket: sweets made from refined sugar.

Page 81
Don Christo Vary: adapted from 'Christopher'.

Cintheas: Cynthia, goddess of the moon and of hunting.

Merop: Merope was loved and carried off by the giant Orion.

This angrie sword: compare *Dr Faustus*, XIII, 73–4: 'And had you cut my body with your swords, / Or hew'd this flesh and bones as small as sand'.

Endnotes

Page 82
Hydraes head: the Hydra was an enormous nine-headed serpent, killed by Hercules as one of his 'twelve labours'.

a champion field: flatten them into open countryside.

Page 83
sownest: soonest.

Page 84
weare: were.

waighty: weighty.

Page 85
blasing starre: a comet, omen of bad fortune.

Page 87
pompered: pampered.

tund: tuned.

Sara: wife of Abraham in the Old Testament.

president: precedent.

Page 88
in a dump: depressed.

Page 89
murrin: plague, disease.

course: curse.

A Pleaſant conceited Hiſtorie, called
The Taming of a Shrew.

Enter a Tapſter, beating out of his doores
Slie Droonken.

Tapſter.

YOu whorſon droonken ſlaue, you had beſt be gone,
And empty your droonken panch ſome where elſe
For in this houſe thou ſhalt not reſt to night.

        Exit Tapſter.

Slie. Tilly vally, by criſee Tapſter Ile feſe you anon.
Fils the tother pot and alls paid for, looke you
I doo drinke it of mine owne Inſtegation,   *Omne bene*
Heere Ile lie a while, why Tapſter I ſay,
Fils a freſh cuſhen heere.
Heigh ho, heers good warme lying.

      He fals aſleepe.

Enter a Noble man and his men
from hunting.

Lord. Now that the gloomie ſhaddow of the night,
Longing to view Orions driſling lookes,
Leapes from th'antarticke World vnto the skie
And dims the Welkin with her pitchie breath,
And darkeſome night oreſhades the chriſtall heauens,
Here breake we off our hunting for to night,

    A 2   Cuppel

Cupple vppe the hounds and let vs hie vs home,
And bid the huntfman fee them meated well,
For they haue all deferu'd it well to daie,
But foft, what fleepie fellow is this lies heere?
Or is he dead, fee one what he dooth lacke? (fleepe,

    Seruingman. My lord, tis nothing but a drunken
His head is too heauie for his bodie,
And he hath drunke fo much that he can go no furder.

    Lord. Fie, how the flauifh villaine ftinkes of drinke.
Ho, firha arife. What fo found afleepe?
Go take him vppe and beare him to my houfe,
And beare him eafilie for feare he wake,
And in my faireft chamber make a fire,
And fet a fumptuous banquet on the boord,
And put my richeft garmentes on his backe,
Then fet him at the *Table* in a chaire:
When that is doone againft he fhall awake,
Let heauenlie muficke play about him ftill,
Go two of you awaie and beare him hence,
And then Ile tell you what I haue deuifde,
But fee in any cafe you wake him not.

    Exeunt two with *Slie.*

Now take my cloake and giue me one of yours,
Al fellowes now, and fee you take me fo,
For we will waite vpon this droonken man,
To fee his countnance when he dooth awake
And finde himfelfe clothed in fuch attire,
With heauenlie muficke founding in his eares,
And fuch a banquet fet before his eies,
The fellow fure will thinke he is in heauen,
But we will be about him when he wakes,
And fee you call him Lord, at euerie word,
And offer thou him his horfe to ride abroad,

                             And

*A*nd thou his hawkes and houndes to hunt the deere,
*A*nd I will aske what futes he meanes to weare,
*A*nd whatfo ere he faith fee you doo not laugh,
But ftill perfwade him that he is a Lord.
    Enter one.
  Mef. And it pleafe your honour your plaiers be com
And doo attend your honours pleafure here.
  Lord. The fitteft time they could haue chofen out,
Bid one or two of them come hither ftraight,
Now will I fit my felfe accordinglie,
For they fhall play to him when he awakes.
  Enter two of the players with packs at their
    backs, and a boy.
Now firs, what ftore of plaies haue you?
  San. Marrie my lord you maie haue a Tragicall
Or a comoditie, or what you will.
  The other. A Comedie thou fhouldft fay, founs
    thout fhame vs all.
  Lord. And whats the name of your Comedie?
  San. Marrie my lord tis calde The taming of a fhrew:
*T*is a good leffon for vs my lord, for vs y̌ are maried men
  Lord. The taming of a fhrew, thats excellent fure,
·Go fee that you make you readie ftraight,
For you muft play before a lord to night,
Say you are his men and I your fellow,
Hees fomething foolifh, but what fo ere he faies,
See that you be not dafht out of countenance.
And firha go you make you ready ftraight,
*A*nd dreffe your felfe like fome louelie ladie,
And when I call fee that you come to me,
For I will fay to him thou art his wife,
Dallie with him and hug him in thine armes,
And if he defire to goe to bed with thee,
    A 3   Then

Then faine some sence and say thou wilt anon.
Be gone I say, and see thou dooft it well.
　Boy. Feare not my Lord, Ile dandell him well enough
And make him thinke I loue him mightilie.　*Ex. boy.*
　Lord. Now firs go you and make you ready to,
For you muft play affoone as he dooth wake.
　San. O braue, firha Tom, we muft play before
A foolifh Lord, come lets go make vs ready,
Go get a difhclout to make cleane your fhooes,
And Ile fpeake for the properties, My Lord, we muft
Haue a fhoulder of mutton for a propertie,
And a little vinegre to make our Diuell rore.
　Lord. Very well: firha fee that they want nothing.
　　　　　　　　　　　　Exeunt omnes.

　　Enter two with a table and a banquet on it, and two
　　　　other, with *Slie* afleepe in a chaire, richlie
　　　　　　apparelled,& the mufick plaieng.
　One. So: firha now go call my Lord,
And tel him that all things is ready as he wild it.
　Another. Set thou fome wine vpon the boord
And then Ile go fetch my Lord prefentlie.　　*Exit*

　　　　Enter the Lord and his men.
　Lord. How now, what is all thinges readie?
　One. I my Lord.　　　　　　　　　(ftraight,
　Lord. Then found the mufick, and Ile wake him
And fee you doo as earft I gaue in charge.
My lord, My lord, he fleepes foundlie: My lord.
　Slie. Tapfter, gis a little fmall ale.　Heigh ho,
　Lord. Heers wine my lord, the pureft of the grape.
　Slie. For which Lord?
　Lord. For your honour my Lord.
　　　　　　　　　　　　　　Slie.